FAITH & FREEDOM

FAITH & FREEDOM

FREEDOM

Toward a Theology
of Liberation

Schubert M. Ogden

Abingdon
Nashville

092244

FAITH AND FREEDOM

Copyright © *1979 by Abingdon*

Library of Congress Cataloging in Publication Data

Ogden, Schubert Miles, 1928-
    Faith and freedom.
    Includes bibliographical references.
    1. Liberation theology—Addresses, essays, lectures. 2.
    Freedom (Theology)—Addresses, essays, lectures. I.
    Title.
    BT83.57.036   261.8   78-12898

ISBN 0-687-125901

MANUFACTURED BY THE PARTHENON PRESS AT
NASHVILLE, TENNESSEE, UNITED STATES OF AMERICA

To
The Lay Theologians
both within and without the churches
who have worked with me
at the theological task

I cannot separate the idea of deliverance from the idea of God, or ever think of man as blessed except as he enters into God's redeeming purpose and labours to make others free.

—Frederick Denison Maurice

CONTENTS

PREFACE

Just before the climax of the Bicentennial Celebration on July 4, 1976, the editors of *The United Methodist Reporter* asked several United Methodist theologians to respond briefly to this question: "In your opinion, what two major theological issues will The United Methodist Church struggle with across the next fifty years?" My response to this question was as follows: First, there is the issue of God, which I formulated in these terms: "Can Christian faith in God be so understood that it positively includes the concern for human liberation in this world?" Then, second, there is the issue of the Christian mission, which I formulated as the question: "Can we understand our special calling as Christians as a new responsibility that we bear for the sake of the world, instead of as a new privilege that only Christians can enjoy?" I recall this here because the origin of this book was in the reflections to which I was led in responding to this question, especially in identifying the first of the two issues with which, in my opinion, the church and theology over the next fifty years will have to struggle.

The purpose of the book, accordingly, is to try to address this first issue in a way that I hope will prove helpful to anyone already struggling with it. This explains why, among other things, I have tried to write for the largest audience I could expect to reach among both laypersons and clergy, assuming a serious interest in understanding how Christian faith in God and the contemporary concern for liberation might be made to interpret one another. I will be pleased, of course, if my professional colleagues are in any way helped by my efforts. But the readers for whom I have primarily written this book are lay theologians of the kind to whom I have taken the liberty of dedicating it.

This has seemed all the more fitting to me because the book has grown out of lectures I gave as the 1977 Laity Week Lectures at Perkins School of Theology. These lectures were then subsequently given, in whole or in part, as the Wertsch Lectures at St. Paul School of Theology in Kansas City, Missouri, the Pollok Lectures at the Atlantic School of Theology in Halifax, Nova Scotia, and the James A. Gray Lectures at the Divinity School of Duke University in Durham, North Carolina. To all of those, mostly lay theologians, who heard these lectures and whose questions and criticisms have been very much in my mind in transforming them into a book, I am grateful. I would also express my thanks to Betty Manning and Mary Ann Marshall, who capably typed the several drafts of the lectures and the book.

Dallas, Texas   S. M. O.

CHAPTER 1

THE CHALLENGE OF THE THEOLOGIES OF LIBERATION

Taken literally and strictly "theology" means *logos* about *theos,* or thought and speech about God. This would seem to indicate that the primary issue for theology at any time must be the issue of God. Certainly, so far as Christian theology is concerned, its first task now and always must be to understand the mystery encompassing our existence to be none other than the God and Father of our Lord Jesus Christ. But it is arguable that, in our own time and for the foreseeable future, the task of thus understanding our existence as encompassed by the reality of God is peculiarly determined by the growing concern for human liberation. This means that if the Christian witness to God is to be understood by persons today, the basic human question to which it must be presented as the answer is the question of liberation—the question as to the real nature of human freedom and its necessary ground. Insofar, then, as theology must always struggle for an understanding of God that is not only appropriate to the Christian witness but also understandable to human existence, the issue with which theology today and tomorrow must above all be concerned is precisely the issue of faith and freedom—of understanding how faith in the God whom we encounter in Jesus Christ is itself the answer to the question of human liberation. Such, at any rate, is the rationale for the present discussion, which is a modest attempt to come to terms with this issue.

Of course, there is nothing new about the

conception of theology's task that I am taking for granted. And it may be helpful in understanding what I am about if we recall the course of development leading up to our present theological situation. I refer to what, speaking broadly, one may call the development of liberal theology.

The origins of liberal theology lie in the realization at roughly the beginning of the nineteenth century that neither the settled orthodoxy of the past nor the then emerging secularism represented a tenable position for Christian theology. With the rise of modern science and the growth of technology, as well as the gradual dawning of historical consciousness, the situation of Western humanity had more and more come to be determined by the new scientific picture of the world and by the resolve of men and women to assume responsibility for their own destinies—using their increasing knowledge and skill to reshape their environment, their society, and themselves. But considering that Christian orthodoxy represented, in effect, a settlement with a prescientific picture of the world, as well as a premodern assessment of the limits of human power and responsibility, one realizes at once why orthodoxy was fundamentally in conflict with the emerging secular self-understanding. Just as clear, however, is why there was an equally basic conflict between Christian faith in God as the primal source and final end of human existence and the kind of secularism for which this world is the only world there is and our liberation of ourselves through historical progress is the only liberation. Thus liberal theology emerged as an attempt by Christian thinkers to bring about a double rapprochement: from the side of a traditional interpretation of the Christian witness toward the modern secular world; and from a wholly secularistic interpretation of modern secularity toward the essential claims of Christian faith.

Such was the project of liberal theology as it was carried out, first of all, in the Protestant theology of the nineteenth century, by figures like Friedrich Schleiermacher and Albrecht Ritschl and then, later on, in Roman Catholic theology, by the so-called Modernists. Notoriously, the main criticism that came to be made of liberal theology was that its attempted reinterpretation of the Christian witness in the terms of modernity resulted in uncritically accommodating that witness to the very different claims of modern secular culture. Yet, significantly, the bearers of this criticism were themselves the heirs of liberal theology, so that it was, in effect, a *self*-criticism. What has commonly been spoken of as neo-orthodoxy—in Protestant theology during the period between the two world wars in the work of men like Karl Barth and Reinhold Niebuhr, and in Catholic theology somewhat later in the work of men like Karl Rahner and Bernard Lonergan—is best understood as the self-critical phase of liberal theology's own continuing development, although there is no denying that there were also reactionary tendencies that avoided uncritically accommodating the witness of faith to the claims of the present only by uncritically preserving the forms of the past.

During the 1950s, however, there were clear signs that theology was moving once again—this time into a genuinely postliberal phase. By this I mean a phase in which the original liberal strategy of double rapprochement, as distinct from modernist accommodation, on the one hand, and fundamentalist preservation, on the other, would determine the shape of theological reflection. Again, speaking broadly, one may say that this is the phase associated with the names of Rudolf Bultmann and Paul Tillich in Protestant theology, and Hans Küng and Edward Schillebeecx in Catholic theology. But here, too, there were unmistakable tendencies toward certain excesses—in this case, toward the out-and-out secularism of the death-of-God theology and associated forms of extreme accommodation to the spirit of the times. It seems fair to say that, at the moment, most theologians have turned their backs on all extremism—in the one direction as well as in the other—and are exploring ways of carrying forward the essential liberal project: a Christian theology that will be, as I like to put it, both appropriate to the Christian witness as it has been handed down to us from the past and understandable to human existence as it has been given to us to live and reflect on in the present.

There is not the least doubt in my mind that it is this overall development of liberal theology, including the genuinely postliberal phase in which it now finds itself, that bears whatever promise there is for the future of Christian theology. Just as certain to me, however, is that what are now commonly called theologies of liberation, which is to say, black theology and the various other ethnic theologies, women's theology, and the theologies of the Third World, all very much belong to this same course of development. They are all examples of a liberal-postliberal type of Christian theology. But to grasp the distinctiveness of these liberation theologies, over against other contemporary examples of the same theological type, it is necessary to recall an important subphase within the larger development of liberal theology that we have just traced—namely, what is usually called "social Christianity," or the "social gospel."

As we have seen, one of the factors of modern secularity, and hence of liberal theology from early on, was a growing historical consciousness, a consciousness that human existence in all its aspects and phases is the process by which men and women make themselves by making their own societies and cultures. Thus existing forms of government, for example, are neither divinely ordained nor naturally given but are historical products of the decisions of men and women in times past as to how their lives should be governed.

This is the truth on which Thomas Paine was so insistent at the time of the American Revolution, when he argued that "although kings are of our creation, they have become the Gods of their creator." By tracing monarchy to its origins in history, Paine exposed it as an all too human institution, with the implication that what human beings had created they could also change. And so he spread the revolutionary insight that forms of government, being historical in origin, are and must be open to revision insofar as they fail to fulfill their proper function of promoting the well-being of those whose lives they govern. In this way, with the emergence of historical consciousness came the ever-clearer realization that to be fully human is to be an active *subject* of historical change, not merely its passive *object.* The clearer this realization became, however, the clearer it also became that most human beings, in most of the important aspects of their lives, neither are nor can be the active subjects of their history. To continue with our same example of forms of government, it became obvious that, in most cases, the decisions by which these forms have been produced have not been the decisions of all whose lives they governed but only of some, the privileged few by whom the fate of the many is by and large determined.

This recognition of fundamental human inequality and injustice, which seemed all the more intolerable the more the already privileged classes proved to be the principal beneficiaries of modern progress, is what gave rise around the middle of the nineteenth century to the movement of social Christianity, or the social gospel. Because the scope of human power and responsibility includes, in principle, the whole social and cultural order, by creating which we create both ourselves and our neighbors, the love for our neighbors as ourselves entailed by faith in the gospel lays upon every Christian responsibility for fundamental change in society and culture themselves—for such structural or systemic change as may be necessary to overcome the inequality and injustice of the existing order. Ever since its emergence, this essential insight of the social gospel has continued to be an important ingredient of liberal theology, even if individual liberal theologies have at times been less concerned with practical issues of action and justice than with more theoretical questions of belief and truth.

It is clearly in the tradition of this same insight that the various theologies of liberation today are to be located, their distinctiveness as liberal theologies lying precisely in their intense preoccupation with the issues of action and justice. Yet it would be mistaken, in my opinion, to see the theologies of liberation as nothing more than a contemporary re-expression of the social gospel. For there is at least this important difference: whereas the social gospel, after all, was typically a movement from within the relatively advantaged human group to take account of the differing historical situations and needs of persons belonging to disadvantaged groups, the theologies of liberation are typically movements within the disadvantaged groups themselves to provide a theological self-interpretation of their own situations and needs. The observation has often been made that it is only after a certain amount of relevant historical progress has already been made by a group that it begins to lay claim to power. The emergence in recent years of the various theologies of liberation—whether black theology, or women's theology, or Third World theology—confirms the soundness of this observation. For these theologies have emerged within the various groups of whose situations and needs they are an attempt at theological interpretation only after these groups have already progressed sufficiently to be more than the passive victims of historical fate. In this connection, the statement of James H. Cone is revealing: "Black Theology is the theological arm of Black Power, and Black Power is the political arm of Black Theology."[1]

This must suffice as a historical introduction to the conception of theology's task that I am here assuming. In all essentials, I have argued, it is the same conception that has been determinative for the whole development of liberal theology from its beginnings right up to our present postliberal situation. I trust it has now also become clear why, in my view, the theologies of liberation that have become so prominent on the contemporary theological scene simply cannot be ignored. As distinctive as they certainly are from other contemporary expressions of a truly liberal theological outlook and approach, these theologies are authentic expressions of essentially the same type of Christian theology; and my conviction is that, with all their limitations, they are among the more forward-looking and hopeful expressions of theology on the present scene.

Why a Challenge—and to Whom?

This brings us to our main topic: the challenge of the theologies of liberation. If one of the necessary conditions of something's being a challenge to someone is that it be in important respects different from anything else that one already is or has, another such condition is that there be at least some respects in which it is also the same. The preceding discussion will presumably have made clear why, so far as I am concerned, there is enough similarity between my own understanding of theology's task and that of the theologies of liberation that they can, indeed, be a challenge at least to me—provided, at any rate, that there are also some respects in which they are sufficiently different. But is there such difference? And who is it, exactly, other than myself, to whom the theologies of liberation are a challenge?

I can best answer these questions by insisting

more than I yet have on the distinction I have already made between witness and theology. I began by saying that, in its strict, literal sense, "theology" means *logos* about *theos,* or thought and speech about God. But in going on, then, to talk about the task of theology, I evidently implied a stricter understanding of theology than simply thought and speech about God in general. For if the task of theology, as I argued, is so to think and speak about God as to be both appropriate to the Christian witness and understandable to human existence, then there is a difference between the thought and speech about God on which theology reflects, which I speak of as Christian witness, and the thought and speech about God in which theology itself is supposed to consist. In other words, what distinguishes theology proper from the thought and speech about God that make up Christian witness generally is that theology is either the process or the product of critically reflecting on that witness with a view to satisfying the twin criteria of appropriateness and understandability.

In general, to reflect is to take something that *appears* to be the case and then to ask more or less deliberately, methodically, and in a reasoned way whether it really is so. Moreover, there is serious reflective work to do whenever something is *said* to be the case. For, first of all, one must determine what is *meant* by what is said—what is meant and what is said are never quite the same—and then, secondly, one must inquire whether what is meant really is the case, in the sense of describing things as they actually are. In saying that theology, properly speaking, is distinct from the witness of faith because it is either the process or the product of critically reflecting on that witness, I mean that theology is the kind of reflection that asks in a deliberate, methodical, and reasoned way about the meaning and truth of the Christian witness of faith.

If we think about it, we realize at once that theology thus understood as reflection on the Christian witness so as to determine its meaning and truth is a necessary task. To be a Christian is to be called to witness to one's faith in and for the world. But, clearly, to determine whether one's witness is adequate, in the sense of being both appropriate and understandable, requires that one engage in theological reflection. More than that, even to become a Christian in the first place requires the same kind of engagement, since one cannot responsibly believe a witness of faith whose meaning one does not understand, nor can one responsibly judge a witness to be true, and therefore worthy of one's belief, unless one feels the force of at least some reasons that may be given for its truth.

To recognize the necessity of theological reflection, however, is also to understand why the task of theology is by no means the task merely of the special group of professionals commonly called theologians. Just as bearing witness to one's faith is the responsibility of every Christian believer, to which each of us is called by our baptism and which we each assume for ourselves with our confirmation, so critically reflecting on the meaning and truth of the Christian witness is also a responsibility that devolves upon every single one of us—and even upon anyone who would responsibly become one of us. I do not in the least mean by this that there are not important differences between being the *lay* theologian to which all Christians are called and being the *professional* theologian to which only some Christians are called, any more than I should question the differences between the lay ministry of every Christian believer and the professional ministry of the church's representative ministers. But, however important the differences between the lay and the professional theologian, they are not more important than those between the lay and the professional minister. The theological task of critically reflecting on one's witness so as to determine its meaning and truth as surely belongs in some way to each of us as Christians as does the ministerial task of somehow bearing that witness by all that we say or do.

Because this is so, there is at least one important respect in which the theologies of liberation are sufficiently different to be a challenge not only to me but to any reader of this book as well. Being reflection on witness rather than witness itself, any such theology simply must be different from, even if in other respects it is the same as, the witness on which it reflects. To this extent, it cannot fail to be a challenge to anyone charged with the responsibility either of bearing the Christian witness or of seriously responding to its claims. This is particularly so because a theology as such differs from witness just insofar as, being either the process or the product of critical reflection on witness, it has to give reasons for its assertions. It is theology at all only because or insofar as it gives reasons for thinking that its claims are both appropriate to the Christian witness and understandable to human existence. But, then, insofar as the theologies of liberation really are theologies in this sense of the word, they are unavoidably a challenge to every Christian responsible for bearing the witness of faith, as well as to any other person who is so much as concerned to understand that witness. For by giving reasons for the appropriateness and understandability of their assertions, these theologies explicitly raise the question of the adequacy of any Christian's witness, and hence are a challenge to him or her, as well as to anyone else who would responsibly decide either to accept or to reject the claim of that witness to be true.

Still, as important as it is to recognize that the theologies of liberation are and must be a challenge to every Christian believer responsible for bearing the witness of faith, this is not the only, or even the primary, respect in which I have ventured to speak of the challenge of these theologies. I maintain that they also pose a challenge to each of us because or insofar as we ourselves are theologians, who, either as laypersons or as professionals, also have the responsibility of critically reflecting on the Christian witness so as to answer the questions of its meaning and truth. Thus I have tried to make clear in the subtitle of this book that it is primarily with respect to our own responsibility to work toward a *theology* of liberation that the theologies of liberation are a challenge to us. Accordingly, it is as one who is himself a theologian speaking to others who, in their ways, are also theologians that I am moved to speak of the challenge of the theologies of liberation.

The Nature of the Challenge

The question now is as to the nature of this challenge. In trying to answer it, I recall my statement about the necessary conditions of something's being a challenge to someone—namely, that it must be, in suitably different respects, both similar to and different from other things that one already is or has or does. This general rule has two corollaries that we need to keep in mind.

First, the similarity that must exist between one's own theological outlook and approach and that typical of the theologies of liberation in order for them to be a challenge need not extend as far as it happens to do in my own case. As I have explained, I myself share with these theologies the general outlook and approach of all liberal theology, according to which there is not simply one criterion of theological adequacy but two—not simply appropriateness to the Christian witness but also understandability to human existence. Even if one does not happen to share this basic outlook and approach, however, one can still be challenged by the theologies of liberation, provided only that there is at least some respect in which one's own way of doing theology and theirs are the same. Such similarity may extend no further, say, than a shared recognition that theology, as reflection on witness, has to be responsible to some criterion or criteria and, consequently, must give good reasons for its assertions.

The second corollary is that the difference that must exist in order for some other theology to be a challenge to our own may take two different forms, either of which suffices to make it is a challenge to us. Specifically, the theologies of liberation can be, and I believe are, a challenge to our own theological efforts both because of what they have already succeeded in doing over against our own failures, and because of what they have as yet failed to do, relative, if not to our own successes, then at least to our resources for doing the same thing more successfully.

The preceding discussion should have made clear what I regard as the main successes of the theologies of liberation. For one thing, they are basically committed to a liberal theological outlook and approach; and, for another, they are intensely preoccupied within that commitment with practical issues of action and justice, as distinct from theoretical questions of belief and truth. Both of these seem to me to be profoundly challenging to much of the theology commonly done among us by professional as well as by lay theologians, just because of our own failures at one or both of these fundamental points. But even with this considerable measure of success, which alone makes them a challenge not only to me but to many others, these theologies also appear to suffer from certain typical failures that make them all the more challenging. This is because they lay upon us the responsibility of so using the resources available to us as to contribute toward overcoming their failures—and, in that sense, to do our own part toward a theology of liberation. As I see it, then, the challenge presented by the various liberation theologies is that of working out a still more adequate theology of liberation than any of them has yet achieved.

To make as clear as possible just wherein this challenge seems to me to lie, I want to identify four points where, as I understand them, the theologies of liberation typically fail to carry out the theological project to which they are committed in an adequate way. I stress the word "typically," for in speaking here and elsewhere in this book of "theologies of liberation," I am speaking of particular theological efforts or positions only insofar as they conform to a certain ideal type. I am quite confident that there are any number of theologies on the present scene that more or less closely conform to this type, and hence could be more or less fairly characterized as "theologies of liberation." But since my purpose here is neither to characterize nor to criticize any particular theology, I make use of this phrase solely to characterize a certain way of doing theology that is more or less represented by any number of theologies but can hardly be exactly identified with any of them—not even those that have characterized themselves by use of this phrase. Moreover, I shall identify the four points where the theologies of liberation have failed by giving four reasons why I, for one, cannot ignore the challenge of trying to work toward a more adequate theology of liberation.

I cannot ignore this challenge, first of all, because *these theologies typically are not so much theology as witness.* The evidence for this is that they tend rather to be the rationalization of positions already taken than the process or the product of critical reflection on those positions. We will have occasion later, in chapter 4, to observe that much the same may be said about the long tradition of Christian theology. The vast majority of theologies have been, in effect if hardly in intention, Christian ideologies, in the precise sense of rationalizing the prior claims of the Christian witness instead of critically inquiring as to their meaning and truth. Be this as it may, it is typical of all the theologies of liberation that they tend to obscure any distinction between theology and witness—not only by what they expressly say about them but even more by what they actually do, or fail to do. Their justification for this, typically, is that theology exists, not for its own sake, but for the sake of the church's witness, its liberating praxis, which theology is supposed to serve. Hence their polemic against so-called academic theology, and their insistence that theology itself must be "engaged," and so on. But, in my view, the issue is not *whether* theology properly serves the praxis of the church as an end beyond itself; the issue, rather, is *how* theology properly performs that service. Does it do so by uncritically assuming that the claims of the Christian witness are true, or that the liberation it promises is one and the same with that for which men and women today are asking? Or is its service to the church's witness the indirect service of critically reflecting on these matters and taking pains to give good reasons for its conclusions concerning them?

I cannot ignore the challenge of the liberation theologies, in the second place, because *they typically focus on the existential meaning of God for us without dealing at all adequately with the metaphysical being of God in himself.* It is the chief defining characteristic of religion generally that, while it is neither simply a metaphysics nor simply an ethics, it is in a peculiar way both. By this I mean that a religion is at once an understanding of ultimate reality as radically other than ourselves and an understanding of our own possibilities of existing and acting in relation to that ultimate reality. Because this is so, theology as the process or the product of critically reflecting on a religion ought ideally to reflect not just one of these two aspects but both of them. But it is a characteristic of the theologies of liberation, consistent with their typical preoccupation with practical issues of action and justice, that they are a reflection more of the ethical, or existential, aspect of the Christian religion than of its metaphysical aspect. In fact, they commonly display a marked impatience with the more theoretical questions of belief and truth, considered simply in themselves in their own right. Their justification for such impatience, typically, is that faith, after all, is more than merely believing certain things about God; for them, faith—being primarily trust in and loyalty to God—necessarily involves existing and acting in a certain way, as distinct from merely holding certain beliefs to be true. But, as I see it, the issue is not *whether* faith in God is primarily an existential matter; the issue, rather, is *how* theology properly takes account of that fact. Does it do so by focusing solely or primarily on the existential meaning of God for our own existence and praxis, even to the point of continuing to assume certain traditional metaphysical beliefs about God uncritically? Or does it begin with faith in its existential meaning for us in order, then, to go on and make fully explicit the metaphysical beliefs about God in himself that faith as such necessarily implies?

I cannot ignore the challenge to work toward a theology of liberation, in the third place, because *the liberation theologies typically tend to confuse—or do not adequately distinguish—two essentially different, though closely related, forms of liberation.* If this book has a single thesis, it is that the one process of liberation whose necessary ground is God comprises two quite different, even if closely related, processes that can and must be distinguished respectively as redemption and emancipation, God himself being understood correspondingly as both the Redeemer and the Emancipator. Consequently, from the standpoint of this thesis, the one thing that any adequate theology of liberation has to avoid is speaking about liberation in merely global, undiscriminating terms, thereby either confusing or failing to distinguish its two irreducibly different forms. And yet nothing is more striking about the theologies of liberation than just such global talk of liberation, with its tacit confusion of redemption with emancipation, of God the Redeemer with God the Emancipator. Indeed, concerned as they are with what they call the praxis of liberation, they are insistent that there is but one process by which human beings are freed from bondage, and they are suspicious of all the usual theological attempts to make any distinctions with respect to that process. They justify such suspicion, typically, by arguing that it is precisely as one integral witness to our own and all other men's and women's freedom from bondage that the Christian witness has been handed down to us from the apostles; and it is this freedom, accordingly, that must be the whole point of theology. But, in my view, the issue is not *whether* there is a single process of liberation that is the whole point of witness and theology; the issue, rather, is *how* theology properly understands that one process. Does it do so by taking liberation to be only or primarily the emancipation from bondage called for by the various movements for human freedom—political, economic, cultural, racial, and sexual? Or does it do so by taking liberation to be primarily the redemption from death, transience, and sin attested by the apostolic witness—and only secondarily, though necessarily, the emancipation from every other form of bondage that redemption itself makes mandatory?

I cannot ignore the challenge of the theologies of liberation, in the fourth place, because *they typically have too restricted or provincial an understanding of the various forms of bondage from which men and women, as well as their fellow creatures, need to be emancipated.* Experience enforces the insight that misery has many forms and that even the best efforts to overcome one of them may be altogether oblivious of others. Thus in a new history of American Communism, a party wife, weary of feeding her husband's comrades, is reported to have finally exploded: "While you sit on your ass making the revolution, *I'm* out there in the kitchen like a slavey. What we need is a revolution in this *house.*"[2] Yet, notwithstanding this insight, each of the theologies of liberation characteristically orients itself to but one form or another of human bondage—political, economic, cultural, racial, or sexual—as though freedom from it were the whole of emancipation. Their justification for this, typically, is that bondage, like freedom, is never to be found merely in general but always and only in just such concrete forms, from which those who suffer the bondage have the right to be freed, even as those of us who can do so have the responsibility of working for their emancipation. But, as I see it, the issue is not *whether* each of these forms of bondage, as well as all of them together is exactly that; the issue, rather, is *how* theology understands this to be the case. Does it do so by supposing that some of them, or all of them together, is *the* bondage that makes emancipation imperative? Or does it try to keep in mind the necessarily multiple forms of bondage, as well as the presence of yet subtler forms than those that most obviously claim our attention and action?

These reasons seem to be more than sufficient to explain why the project of a theology of liberation is the challenge put to the rest of us by the already existing theologies that bear this name. If this implies that these theologies have not wholly succeeded in what they themselves have projected—for at least the reasons I have given—it also implies that the project itself is a challenge to the best we have to offer as theologians. The task before us, therefore, is to join in the project and to make our own contribution to it—confident not only that there is room for anything we have to contribute, but also that the instrinsic worth of the project will justify even the most modest contribution we can offer.

In taking up this challenge, as I propose to do in the chapters that follow, I would underscore the indications already given that our task here is limited to moving *toward* a theology of liberation and that taking a few important steps in that direction is all we can hope to do. My comments just now about the necessarily multiple forms of bondage and the presence of subtler forms than we commonly recognize will have made clear that I envisage the possibility of other, rather different theologies of liberation from those that already exist. But it should also have become clear that any such theology would not be *the,* but only *a* theology of liberation. There would still be room, just as there is now, for many other such theologies. Nevertheless, it seems to me that any theology of liberation that were at all adequate would share with every other in the same fundamental understanding of faith in God, given the basic human question of freedom. Consequently, our most urgent theological task, as I see it, is to clarify just this fundamental theological understanding. It is to this important, even if limited, task that the two succeeding chapters are devoted.

CHAPTER 2

FAITH AS THE EXISTENCE OF FREEDOM: IN FREEDOM FOR FREEDOM

The challenge of the theologies of liberation, I have argued, is to join them in working toward a still more adequate understanding of faith and freedom than any of them has already managed to achieve. Such a project remains to be carried out because, for various reasons, the existing liberation theologies typically have not yet succeeded in realizing it. Thus, whether because they are not so much theology as witness, or because they stress the meaning of God for us without dealing adequately with the being of God in himself, or because they tend to confuse the liberation that is redemption with the liberation that is emancipation, or finally because they have too provincial an understanding of the forms of bondage from which some or all of us need to be emancipated—whether for one or more of these reasons, the liberation theologies already on the scene have typically failed to develop the kind of theology of liberation that is clearly indicated.

In now taking up their challenge to contribute toward such a theology, I shall be concerned, in this chapter and the next, with what I have called the fundamental theological understanding that any adequate theology of liberation would perforce share with every other. Specifically, I shall be concerned with clarifying the essential meaning of Christian faith in God, assuming that the question in terms of which such faith is to be understood is the question asked by men and women today concerning the nature and ground of human freedom.

Two further comments are necessary to introduce the argument of these chapters.

It should be evident by now that, as I view the task of Christian theology, the first concern of the theologian must always be to achieve a reflective understanding of the Christian witness that is appropriate to that witness itself. But this obviously raises the question of how the criterion of appropriateness thus acknowledged is actually to be applied. How, exactly, does one go about determining what is and is not appropriate theology? What is the standard or norm of such appropriateness?

Historically, Protestant theology has replied to this question by pointing to Scripture, especially the New Testament. Although Protestants have been clear right from the beginning that the sole ultimate source of theological authority is Jesus Christ himself, who, as Luther liked to say, is "king of Scripture" *(rex scripturae),* they have also been insistent that the Christ who is, indeed, king even of Scripture can be none other than the Christ of whom Scripture alone is the primary witness. It is in this sense that they have traditionally upheld the principle "Scripture *alone*" *(sola scriptura),* as over against the traditional Roman Catholic appeal to "Scripture *and* tradition," which is to say, Scripture and the *magisterium,* or teaching office of the church, epitomized in the infallible teaching office of the Pope. But one of the consequences of the historical-critical study of Scripture, which is perhaps the greatest single achievement of liberal theology, is the recognition that even the writings comprised in the canon of the New Testament are not original witness to Christ, and hence not properly apostolic. On the contrary, because they all evidently make use of sources earlier than themselves, they are all more or less later interpretations of the apostolic witness, which was historically prior to them and must now be reconstructed from them. In other words, the historic Protestant insistence on Scripture alone as primary norm over against all tradition has now become untenable because the writings of Scripture themselves are now known to be—precisely tradition!

I have not thought to mention this important consequence of scriptural study in order to go into all the difficulties it raises, much less to try to deal with them. But it has seemed to me of some importance to explain why I myself am no longer able to give the reply to the question of the standard or norm of theological appropriateness that Protestant theologians have traditionally given. Were I to give adequate reasons for thinking that the assertions I shall make about faith and freedom are, in fact, appropriate to the Christian witness, I should feel bound to appeal not simply to Scripture, or even to the New Testament, but to what I understand to be the true apostolic and, therefore, canonical witness. I refer to the earliest layer of witness now accessible to us through historical-critical study of the Synoptic Gospels, which, following one of the most careful students of this whole matter, Willi Marxsen, I call the Jesus-kerygma.[3] Ever since the canon of Scripture was gradually decided by the early church, the true standard or norm of canonicity, and hence of all Christian witness and theology, has been the witness of the apostles, in the sense of the original witness to Jesus as the Christ upon which all other Christian witness and theology, as well as all Christian faith, necessarily depend. But if we today, given our own historical methods and knowledge, are to continue to submit our assertions to this same standard or norm, we have no choice but to locate it, not in the New Testament writings as we now have them, but in this earliest kerygma, or witness to Jesus, that we are now able to reconstruct by critical study of the Gospels. Consequently, even though I shall not be able to show at all adequately how the assertions I shall make do, in fact, measure up to this norm, it is on the basis of my continuing study of the Jesus-kerygma that I shall be making these assertions, and it is precisely to it, as the true Christian canon, that I should feel obliged to appeal, finally, in giving reasons for them.

The other introductory comment I have to make is by way of explaining the rationale of these two central chapters. I have argued that theologians today are called to work out a theology of liberation because or insofar as it is in terms of the question of freedom that men and women today typically ask the existential question concerning the ultimate meaning of their existence. Behind this argument is my assumption that it is precisely this existential question, whether in terms of freedom or some other terms, that is the religious and, therefore, theological question. Implied by this assumption is that religious assertions generally, and, consequently, the assertions of Christian witness and theology in particular, are existential assertions, in that, whatever else they may be about, they are always concerned with our own possibilities of existing and acting in the world, and hence give answer in some way or other to this existential question.

To be sure, I have already said enough in criticizing the theologies of liberation to make clear why no theology can legitimately focus solely on the existential meaning of God for us, to the exclusion of all considerations of the metaphysical being of God in himself. Not only the Christian religion but any religion has by its very nature a metaphysical as well as an existential aspect. Consequently, if religious assertions are always about our own possibilities of existing and acting, and are to that extent existential, they are never about nothing other than our own possibilities, because they are also always about the ultimate reality apart from which we could neither exist nor act at all, and so are also metaphysical. In fact, the most careful analyses of religious language by both social scientists and philosophers have again and again confirmed that the chief defining characteristic of a religious assertion is that it is about our own existence in the world only in relation to the ultimate reality that is its primal source and final end—and vice versa.

Because this is so, theological reflection on religious assertions—or in the case of Christian theology, on the assertions comprising the Christian witness of faith—can assume no other form than an explication of the existential meaning of God for us as both implying and implied by an explication of the metaphysical being of God in himself. It is just because, on the basis of the apostolic witness, we understand the ultimate reality encompassing our existence to be in itself the God whom Jesus calls Father that we both can and should understand ourselves in the world in the distinctive way in which that witness summons us to do. But the converse statement is also true, that it is just because, on the basis of the same apostolic witness, we both can and should understand our existence in the world in this distinctive way that we must understand the primal source and final end of our existence to be none other than the God and Father of Jesus Christ.

This is the reason, then, for the structure and movement of the argument in this chapter and the next, which are devoted respectively to these two mutually dependent explications: of the meaning of God for us, and of the being of God in himself. Accordingly, what is said in either chapter can be rightly understood only by taking account of what is also said in the other. At the same time, I would insist that the order of the two explications is by no means arbitrary, since there are the best of reasons in the very nature of faith itself for beginning with the existential meaning of God for us before going on to explicate the metaphysical being of God in himself.

Faith as Existence in *Freedom*

Our first question, then, is about the existential meaning of faith in God, given the contemporary concern for human freedom. The answer I shall give to this question is the one summarized in the title of this chapter: Faith is the existence of freedom. By this I mean, quite simply, that the distinctive way of understanding ourselves in the world that is properly described as Christian faith in God is a way of existing and acting *in* freedom and *for* it. This answer must now be unpacked, and I begin with the first assertion it involves, that faith in God is existence *in* freedom.

No doubt the principal difficulty in accepting, if not, indeed, in understanding, this assertion is the long-standing and widespread tendency within the church and without it to identify faith with belief, or, more accurately, with *belief about,* as distinct from *belief in.* This tendency is evident from a very early time in the life of the church, as is clear from the polemical claim of the Letter of James in the New Testament that "faith apart from works is dead" (2:26). As every good Protestant is aware, this claim has always been a problem, since it seems so obviously to conflict with the characteristic claim of Paul that "a man is justified by faith alone apart from works of the law" (Rom. 3:28). But one of the results of the continuing historical-critical study of Scripture is the conviction, now widely shared by New Testament scholars, that James' polemic is not really directed against Paul's own understanding of faith and justification but, rather, against a very different understanding of faith, according to which it means believing certain things about God, in the sense of sincerely holding them to be true. For Paul himself, on the contrary, faith is understood primarily as obedient submission to the gift and demand of God's grace, and hence as belief in God himself, in the twofold sense of trust in his love and loyalty to its cause. Thus the only faith that Paul understands to be a justifying faith is not the mere belief *about* God that James has in mind when he hears the word "faith," but, rather, that belief *in* God that, as Paul himself puts it, is always and of necessity "faith working through love" (Gal. 5:6).

Far from conflicting with Paul's view, then, James' insistence that works are necessary to justification is by way of making the very point that Paul himself would undoubtedly have wanted to make, had he assumed James' different understanding of faith as

mere belief *about* God, instead of what he in fact
does assume, namely, that faith is primarily belief *in*
God and hence fidelity to his love as well as
confidence in it. It seems worth remarking in passing
that it is from just this sort of example that one can
learn from the New Testament itself that the
church's teachers and theologians have always
recognized that making statements appropriate to
what the apostolic witness *means* is something
different and more demanding than merely repeat-
ing what it *says.* James would certainly have done
far worse a job in bearing the witness of faith than he
in fact did if he had continued to use Paul's words in
a situation in which they could no longer be
understood to mean what Paul himself meant by
them.

This tendency, already evident in the New
Testament, to interpret faith as only, or primarily, a
matter of believing certain things to be true, was all
the more strongly reinforced the more the church
moved out of its original Jewish environment and
sought to understand its witness in a Hellenistic
religious and cultural context. Indeed, the classic
definitions of "faith" in patristic and medieval
theology make clear that this is the interpretation of
faith that increasingly came to prevail in the church.
Nor was the Reformers' vigorous attempt to reintro-
duce the earlier and more scriptural understanding
of faith as belief in God, and hence as trust in his love
and loyalty to him, sufficient to keep even the

Protestant churches and theology from once again succumbing to the same tendency. Consequently, right up to today, persons both within the church and without it commonly understand the faith in God to which the Christian witness is the summons as primarily, if not only, a matter of believing certain things about God—namely, those things that they understand to comprise proper Christian belief, whether orthodox or otherwise.

As long as this common understanding of faith prevails, my assertion that faith in God is existence in freedom is not likely to seem true. For that matter, it will hardly even be understood. Nevertheless, there are few things a theologian can say more confidently than that the understanding of faith as primarily belief about God has no warrant whatever either in Scripture or, more importantly, in the apostolic witness that is the norm even of the claims of Scripture. Just when one orients oneself to theology's primary source in Scripture and to its apostolic norm, it becomes clear beyond any question that Christian faith in God, in its primary sense, is an existential matter of believing *in* God, as distinct from an intellectual matter of believing certain things *about* God.

It is true that this primary sense of "faith" is not its only sense—not even in Scripture or in the witness of the apostles—and that the distinction on which I have insisted between belief in God and belief about God ought never to be construed as implying their

separation. Contrary to David Hume, not everything
that can be distinguished can be separated, and this
is nowhere more obvious, or important, than in this
matter of the two senses of "faith." To trust in God's
love as it is decisively re-presented to us in Jesus
Christ, or to be loyal to his love by loving him and, in
him, all whom he loves, is clearly to presuppose that
the mystery encompassing our existence really is the
God who, quite apart from our own trust and loyalty,
loves both us and all our fellow creatures. Consequently, unless these beliefs about God were
true—unless ultimate reality really were the God of
all-embracing love—there clearly would be no point
whatever either in our trusting in his love or in our
being faithful to him. Even so, the inseparability of
belief *in* God from belief *about* God should in no
way obscure the fact that the first is the primary
sense of "faith" in the normative witness of the
apostles, as well as in Scripture generally. The
justifying faith in God attested by Paul and
rediscovered by the Reformers is, first of all, trust in
the promise of God's love declared to us in Jesus
Christ and loyalty to the cause of God's love that all
things be brought to their proper fulfillment, to his
glory.

It is to faith thus understood, then, that my
assertion is intended to refer when I say that faith in
God is existence *in* freedom. And the reason for this
assertion, as what I have already said will have

indicated, is this: According to the normative Christian witness, the mystery encompassing our existence as its primal source and final end, whence it comes and whither it goes, is none other than God—specifically, the God and Father of our Lord Jesus Christ, who is the pure, unbounded love of all things and the Father of every man and woman. Because it is in this God's all-embracing love that all things have their beginning and end, and because there is nothing whatever that can separate us from his love—not even death and transience, or our own sinful forgetfulness of its presence—because it is this love that ever was, is, and remains our only final end, even as it is our only primal source, we are one and all presented in every moment of our lives with the gift and demand of faith. This is to say that we are continually presented with the gift and demand of utterly trusting in God's love as the only ultimate ground of our own being and meaning, as well as of the being and meaning of everything else, and of being utterly loyal to this same love as the only cause inclusive enough in its concern for the fulfillment of all things to claim all our love and service.

Of course, the gift and demand of faith in God are decisively *re*-presented to us in Jesus Christ as we encounter him through the Christian witness of faith. What we as Christians mean by "Jesus Christ" is the event in our common human history that is both the origin and the principle of our own faith in God and witness to him and is originally attested as such in the normative witness of the apostles. This means that the Jesus to whom we bear witness as the Christ is the decisive re-presentation, or presenting again through concepts and symbols, of the same gift and demand of faith in God that never cease to be present in our actual existence as long as we exist and act humanly at all. Conversely, it means that the possibility of faith in God implicitly presented to each of us in our actual existence is none other than the possibility of faith in God explicitly re-presented to all of us in Jesus Christ.

But faith understood as an existence in utter trust in God's love and utter loyalty to his cause as they are decisively revealed in Christ can only be an existence in freedom—and that in two distinct, albeit closely related senses of the word.

Faith is existence in freedom, in the first place, in the negative sense of *freedom from*—freedom *from* all things, ourselves and the world, as in any way essential to determining the ultimate meaning of our lives. Because faith, as we have seen, is, first of all, utter trust in the love of God as the primal source and final end of our own unique existence, as well as of everything else, to exist in faith is to be freed from any compulsion to find the ultimate ground of one's life in something else alongside God. Being bound utterly and completely to God, the believer is utterly and completely freed from everything else. Indeed, the believer exists in the knowledge that, no matter what happens, good or bad, it is finally indifferent or of no consequence insofar as we always exist under God's loving care and, together with all our fellow creatures, are finally safe—in the sense that our lives, like theirs, are embraced within God's boundless and everlasting love, where they have an abiding meaning in spite of our own death and sin and the transience of all things. Because the mystery encompassing our existence is the limitless acceptance of God's love, faith as the acceptance of that acceptance, and, in that sense, as trust in God's love, is existence in freedom *from* literally everything else.

For the very same reason, faith is existence in freedom, in the second place, in the positive sense of *freedom for*—freedom *for* literally everything else, ourselves and the world, as all worthy of our own love and devoted service. Just because faith is, first of all, utter trust in God's love for us, to exist in faith is to be freed from ourselves and the world and, at one and the same time, also to be freed for them. It is existence in freedom in this second or positive sense that is actualized by our faith insofar as it is not only trust in God's love but also loyalty to God and, therefore, also to all those to whom he himself is loyal—which means, of course, literally everyone. Thus, being bound utterly and completely to God, the believer is utterly and completely freed for everything else. Indeed, the believer exists in the knowledge that all that happens, good or bad, is so far from being indifferent or of no consequence as to give concrete content or direction to our own responsibility to care—to care for all those who are or become our neighbors and, by serving their creaturely needs, to optimize the limits of their freedom to become fully themselves. Just because the mystery encompassing our lives is God's boundless acceptance, faith as the trusting acceptance of that acceptance is also the freedom to accept all those whom God accepts and, therefore, is existence in freedom *for* all things, our fellow creatures as well as ourselves.

Faith as Existence for *Freedom*

This understanding of faith as existence in freedom, in the positive sense of freedom *for* ourselves and the world, as well as in the negative sense of freedom *from* them, is nothing new in Christian theology. As a matter of fact, to this extent, there has been an explicit theology of liberation ever since the New Testament; for it is in these very terms, of freedom from and freedom for all things, that Paul, notably, explicates the whole meaning of existence in faith—making use in doing so of the Stoic concept of "freedom" *(eleutheria),* which, having no precedent in the Old Testament and Judaism, allowed for a novel theological explication of the meaning of faith in God. Thus Paul can write to the Corinthians, "Now the Lord is the Spirit, and where the Spirit of the Lord is, there is freedom" (2 Cor. 3:17), just as he can attest to the Galatians, "For freedom Christ has set us free; stand fast therefore, and do not submit again to a yoke of bondage" (Gal. 5:1). Not surprisingly, the Protestant Reformers, who were so extensively dependent on Paul, characteristically interpreted Christian existence precisely as existence in freedom—the classic of all such interpretation being Luther's treatise *The Freedom of a Christian,* in which he summarizes all that it means to be a Christian in the two paradoxical statements: "A Christian is a perfectly free lord of all, subject to none," and "A Christian is a perfectly dutiful servant of all, subject to all."[4]

This second statement that the Christian who exists in perfect freedom is at the same time a dutiful servant, bound to the service of everyone, already opens up the other thing we must consider in this chapter. It is Luther himself whose support I can claim in making the second assertion implied by my title—namely, that faith is also existence *for* freedom. In making this assertion, I particularly have in mind another statement of Luther's, to the effect that "the first and highest work of love that a Christian ought to do once he has come to believe is that he should bring others to faith even as he himself has come to it." Luther's point is obvious enough: to exist in faith is to do the works of love; and the first and highest of such works is to open up for others, also, the possibility of existing in faith.

But if we now reflect on this point in the light of the conclusion we have just reached, that the possibility of existing in faith can be nothing other than the possibility of existing in freedom, in freedom *from* all things and in freedom *for* them, then the force of Luther's point, clearly, is that the faith that is existence *in* freedom is, by its very nature, also existence *for* freedom—for the freedom of all the others, for whom the Christian is freed to live through utterly trusting in God's love.

We may be quite sure that what Luther had in mind in saying that the first and highest work of love is to bring others to faith even as we ourselves have come to it is that the Christian's preeminent responsibility is to bear witness to the grace of God in Jesus Christ. Certainly, in Luther's view, the only one who can bring any person to faith in the strict sense of the words is God himself as he encounters us in Christ, through the Holy Spirit. For it is God's prevenient grace of accepting our lives into his own that is the necessary condition of the possibility of our accepting his acceptance through faith. There-fore, the only way in which we as Christians could possibly bring others to faith is to bear witness to them of God's redeeming love, which must itself be the only ultimate ground of their faith even as it is of our own. What Luther's point comes to, then, is that the first and highest work of any Christian who exists in freedom is to bear witness to others of the boundless love of God, whose meaning for them is the gift and demand of the same radical freedom.

This raises the question of just how the Christian is to bear such witness. Ordinarily, the term "witness" is understood in a fairly strict sense to refer to specific words and deeds having explicitly to do with the redeeming love of God in Jesus Christ. Thus the paradigms of witness are all assumed to be specifically religious, being, first of all, the church's explicit proclamation of Christ through its preaching and sacraments and, dependent thereon, the explicit testimony of individual Christians to God's redeeming love. But while this assumption certainly is understandable, it is mistaken, in my opinion, to suppose that the only Christian witness is the explicit witness that constitutes the Christian religion. It is characteristic of any religion, including Christianity, that it neither is nor can be the only witness to the faith of which it is the most explicit primary expression. The reason for this is that the same faith that is *explicitly* expressed through the specific cultural forms of religion is and must be *implicitly* expressed through all the other cultural forms—morality and politics, technology and the arts. Because this is so, there is not only the *explicit* Christian witness that is properly borne through specifically religious words and deeds but also the *implicit* Christian witness that can and should be borne through every nonreligious word and deed as well.

In this connection, I always recall a statement of

Alexander Miller, that "to give men bread is not to affirm that they live by bread alone, but to witness that we do not."[5] I submit that the witness in such a case goes even further, attesting to other persons that, in the final analysis, they do not live by bread alone, either. In this way, not only our explicit Christian witness to Jesus as the Christ but also whatever we say or do to meet even the most ordinary human need always witnesses to the love of God as the gift and demand of just that existence *in* freedom which is also existence *for* the freedom of others.

I will not venture to judge to what extent Luther might have concurred in this insistence that there is an implicit as well as an explicit Christian witness. When he speaks of bearing witness as "the first and highest work of love that a Christian ought to do," his implication, clearly, is that there are also other works of love, even if they are all secondary to and lower than the one preeminent work of bringing others to faith. Obviously, one way of understanding this implication would be to suppose that Luther assumes something like the same distinction I have made here in order to represent bearing explicit witness to Christ as the first and highest work of a Christian, relative to the implicit witness constituted by all the other works of love. But my guess is that this would be to overinterpret Luther's meaning, reading into his statement a distinction he hardly assumes. In any case, I should myself prefer to see a somewhat different point in the statement, whether or not Luther himself ever intended to make it.

As it happens, it is the same kind of point that he himself makes elsewhere in his interpretation of the Ten Commandments, when he takes the First Commandment to be first in another and deeper sense than simply being first in an ordinal series. Rightly understood, he argues, the First Commandment is the *only* commandment, since it calls for that whole and undivided trust in God and loyalty to him that comprise all of human obedience. Thus Luther insists that it is precisely faith that is the fulfillment of the First Commandment, even as sin is its transgression, and he interprets the other nine commandments as all entirely dependent for their force on it, being in effect, specific ways of expressing the one demand that we trust solely in God and be faithful to none but him. My conviction is that it is in the very same way that we should understand what Luther means when he speaks of the "first and highest work of love that a Christian ought to do." The bearing witness to God's grace to which he undoubtedly refers is not merely one work of love alongside all the others, even if the first and highest. Rather, its being the first and highest means that it is rightly understood as the *only* work of love, the one work to which the other works are all supposed to contribute, being, in effect, specific ways of bearing witness to God's strictly universal work of love. Thus, as important as it is to insist on the implicit as well as the explicit form of Christian witness, it is even more important to recognize that the witness to God's love of which both are forms is not merely one work of love among others but comprises all the works of love that a Christian ought to do.

This means, then, that the whole of Christian existence may be said to be an existence for freedom. If all the works of love are comprised in bearing witness to the love of God, and if the whole point of such witness is to attest to the ground of others' freedom as well as our own, then "existence for freedom" applies to all that Christians say and do, not merely to some of it. Of course, Luther's own way of putting the matter reminds us that all that a Christian ought to do is covered by the phrase, "the works of love." To exist in faith is not only to trust in God's faithfulness to us but also to be faithful to him, and that means to be faithful as well to all those to whom he is faithful. But to be faithful to God and to all to whom he is faithful is precisely what it means to love them, just as God's love for us is nothing other than his faithfulness to us. So we can understand exactly what Paul means when he speaks of "faith working through love." Unless I am mistaken, however, the one test of whether love is really present is always freedom—both in the sense that the test of whether one loves another is always whether one intends to speak and act in such a way as somehow to optimize the limits of the other's freedom, and in the sense that the test of whether one is loved by another is always whether the limits of one's own freedom are in some respect thus optimized by what the other says and does.

But if the test of love's real presence in both of these senses is always freedom, there can be no doubt whatever that faith is existence for freedom as well as in freedom. For if anything is certain about faith, to judge from Scripture and its apostolic norm, it is that to exist in faith is to exist in love: love of God and, in God, of all those whom he himself already loves.

The conclusion of this chapter, then, is that faith in God is indeed the existence of freedom in the twofold sense that it is both existence *in* freedom and existence *for* freedom. Because faith is utter trust in God's love as well as utter loyalty to him and his cause, it is both the negative freedom *from* all things and the positive freedom *for* all things—to love and to serve them by so speaking and acting as to respond to all their creaturely needs. In this respect faith is existence *in* freedom, and so a *liberated* existence—an existence liberated by God's redeeming love. But because faith is utter loyalty to God and his cause as well as utter trust in him, it is also existence *for* freedom, and so also a *liberating* existence—an existence devoted to so bearing witness to God's love by all that we say and do as to optimize the limits of others' freedom in whatever ways this can be done.

The discussion will have already indicated that there are, in fact, two basic ways in which what we can say or do can optimize the limits of others' freedom by bearing witness to them of God's love. There is, first of all, the way of bearing explicit witness to the redeeming love of God re-presented in Jesus Christ, which is the only ultimate ground of all others' liberation as surely as it is of our own. Then, secondly, there is the way of bearing implicit witness to God's love which consists in saying and doing all the countless other things that answer to creaturely needs, and hence also optimize the limits of freedom. In the next chapter, I shall argue that these two basic ways in which our words and deeds can optimize the limits of freedom are, in fact, our ways of participating in God's own liberating work—both his redeeming and his emancipating work. But all that I need underscore here is that the liberating existence, or existence for freedom, that is of the essence of faith in God is itself not simple but complex—or, rather, duplex—being, as we shall presently see, a participation in both the redemption and the emancipation that together constitute the liberating work of God.

CHAPTER 3

GOD AS THE GROUND OF FREEDOM: THE REDEEMER & THE EMANCIPATOR

Our task in these chapters is to contribute toward a more adequate theology of liberation than has as yet been achieved and to do so by working out the understanding fundamental to such a theology. This means that our central concern is so to clarify the essential meaning of Christian faith in God that it can be understood to be the answer to the question of freedom. Thus we have recognized that the primary terms of our discussion are "faith" and "freedom," and in the preceding chapter it became clear that the second term may indeed be used to interpret the meaning of the first—to the point, in fact, of allowing us to say that existence in faith *is* the existence of freedom, in the twofold sense of existence *in* freedom and existence *for* freedom.

But it will also have become clear that if the meaning of "faith" may thus be understood in terms of "freedom," this is only because or insofar as the meaning of "freedom" may itself be interpreted in terms of "faith"—with the result that, if faith in God may be said to be the existence of freedom, one may also say that the only authentic existence of freedom is faith in God. In this way, the question of men and women today concerning the nature and ground of human freedom is answered by transforming it in terms of Christian faith's own essential witness to the God whose service is perfect freedom.

This explains why, having explicated the meaning of God for us, we must now proceed to explicate the being of God in himself. If the only authentic existence of freedom is faith in God, the question concerning the nature of freedom is inseparable from the question concerning its ground, and it is only when the second question has also been answered that the answer already given to the first will itself be fully explicit. Of course, the starting point for this second explication is one and the same with that for the first—namely, the Christian witness of faith to Jesus as the Christ, understood by reference to its apostolic norm. Just as that witness is the re-presentation to everyone whom it encounters of the possibility of faith in God's love as the gift and demand of radical freedom—of existence *in* freedom and *for* freedom—so it is also, at one and the same time, the assertion that the mystery encompassing our existence is the God whom Jesus addressed as Father, and so nothing other than pure unbounded love. Consequently, even as the explication of existence in faith in the preceding chapter could not be carried out except by constantly referring to its ground in the being and action of God himself, so the explication that must be undertaken here of the being and action of God cannot be achieved except by constantly referring to our own possibility of existing and acting in faith. Even so, there is an important difference of emphasis between the one task and the other, and it is only after both have been carried out that we will have achieved the fundamental understanding that any theology of liberation must share.

This needs to be emphasized all the more strongly, since, as I argued in chapter 1, this is one of the points where the already existing theologies of liberation have been notably unsuccessful. Presumably because they are so intensely preoccupied with the admittedly urgent issues of action and justice, as distinct from questions of belief and truth, they tend to be far more successful in explicating the meaning of God for us—for our own liberating praxis, as they typically say—than in explicating the being of God in himself. As a matter of fact, aside from certain notable exceptions among the Roman Catholic liberation theologians working in Latin America—I am thinking especially of Juan Luis Segundo—the liberation theologies are characteristically lacking in anything that could be called a "theology" in the strict and proper sense of an adequately developed doctrine of God. Typically, they ignore altogether the questions of fundamental theology concerning the concept and existence of God, and even the more properly systematic theological questions of the being and action of God they tend to deal with only incidentally in the course of explicating the meaning of God for us as the gift and demand of freedom. Not surprisingly, therefore, the existing theologies of liberation typically show signs of still being very much under the influence of a metaphysical understanding of God that has played a fateful role in Christian theology. Because they fail to do their own metaphysical thinking consistently with what they themselves take to be the existential meaning of faith in God, they tend simply to perpetuate uncritically the well-known concept of God of classical metaphysics.

I say there is nothing surprising about this because the only alternative to a good metaphysics, when one undertakes to explicate the beliefs about God implicit in the Christian witness, is a bad metaphysics; and one of the ways of virtually insuring that one's metaphysics will be bad is to take it over incidentally and uncritically instead of deliberately and reflectively. In fact, not even a deliberate and reflective approach to the metaphysical question of the being and action of God in himself is sufficient if one allows one's consideration to be confined to too restricted a range of metaphysical alternatives. This becomes almost poignantly apparent in the case of as good a book as Segundo's *Our Idea of God*.[6] Even though, unlike most liberation theologians, Segundo is very definitely concerned to work out a metaphysical understanding of God and, moreover, is well aware that classical metaphysical theism simply will not do, his acquaintance with the real alternatives for doing this and with all the resources that are actually available is so limited that his project is doomed to fail right from the outset. Naturally, no one can be held accountable for knowing more than one is able to know. But anyone who does know more, or, at any rate, thinks one does, certainly is accountable for extending the range of alternatives for reasoned choice and for employing such other resources as are, in fact, available.

Here I must simply confess that I think those of us who are acquainted with certain other contemporary expressions of a genuinely postliberal theology can very well be held accountable for doing exactly this. This seems to me particularly true of any of us who are familiar with so-called process theology, as well as the "process philosophy" lying behind it. In fact, I am confident that it is precisely the metaphysics that has been worked out by certain of the process philosophers—notably, Alfred North Whitehead and Charles Hartshorne—that goes beyond all the usual metaphysical alternatives and provides the very resources that are required if the project of a theology of liberation is to be carried out to completion.

The reason I can speak with such confidence is that one of the ways—and, in my opinion, the most adequate way—of describing what process metaphysics is all about is to say that it is the metaphysics that takes "freedom" as its key concept. I should explain that, as I am using the term here, "metaphysics" refers to that form of critical reflection which seeks to make fully explicit and understandable the most fundamental presuppositions of all our experience and thought, or, as I may also say, the most universal principles that are the strictly necessary conditions of the possibility of anything whatever.

Because these presuppositions or principles are radically more fundamental or universal than any other, they can be understood in terms of our ordinary concepts only by analogy, or by generalizing these concepts well beyond the limits of their ordinary uses. Thus one metaphysics differs from another primarily because of the concepts, especially the key concept, it chooses to generalize and because of the consistency or thoroughness of its generalizations. What I should say about process metaphysics, then, is that it differs from every other because of the consistent and thoroughgoing way in which it generalizes the key concept of "freedom."

Of course, one might well suppose from the title usually given to it that it is rather "process" that must be the key concept of process metaphysics. But the reply to such a supposition is that what the process philosophers I have in mind mean when they use the concept "process" is simply the process of creative synthesis, or self-creation, whereby whatever becomes actual does so only by freely synthesizing into a new unity the multiplicity of data provided by the free self-creations of others. In other words, for process metaphysics, to be anything actual at all is to be a free response to other freedom—or, more exactly, to the results of other freedom in the form of the many other things themselves already actual. Because this is so, one may go so far as to say that process metaphysics is precisely *the* metaphysics of freedom, which insists

on the applicability of its key concept to literally
everything that can be actual at all, from the least
particle of so-called physical matter to the God than
whom, in Anselm's words, "none greater can be
conceived."

The Concept of God in Process Metaphysics

So that it will become even clearer why process
metaphysics is just the metaphysics that an adequate theology of liberation requires, I want to
characterize briefly how it generalizes the concept of
freedom and thereby achieves a distinctive understanding of ultimate reality, and hence of the reality
of God. I will also try to show that the significance of
this general understanding of things for Christian
theology is directly due to its differing at two
absolutely critical points from the traditional metaphysics presupposed by classical Christian theism.

The characteristic claim of process metaphysics, I
have said, is that to be anything actual at all, whether
the least such thing that can be conceived or the
greatest, is to be an instance of process, or creative
synthesis, and, therefore, a free response to the free
decisions of others already made. This means that
anything actual both freely creates itself by responding to the self-created others already actualized and belonging to its past and then contributes
itself, along with those others, to the still other

self-creations as yet unactualized and belonging to its future. But if this be the metaphysical nature of things, and thus of anything that is so much as coherently conceivable, two consequences follow that are of critical theological importance.

In the first place, it follows that *nothing whatever, not even God, can wholly determine the being of something else.* Taken in a completely generalized, analogical sense, "freedom" means self-creation and, therefore, determination by self in contrast to determination by others. Assuming, then, as process metaphysics maintains, that freedom in this sense is a strictly universal metaphysical principle, one must infer that anything that is even conceivably actual is and must be, in its own way or to its own degree, self-created. This need not mean and, as we shall see, must not mean that self-creation ever occurs in the complete absence of creation by others, any more than creation by others ever occurs in the complete absence of creation by self. But since it clearly belongs to the very idea of freedom as self-creation to exclude being completely determined by others, what anything is, is always, in part, the result of its own free decision, as distinct from the decisions of others that it must somehow take into account.

This implies, then, that even the greatest conceivable power over others—the "omnipotent" power than which none greater can be conceived—could not be all the power there is. Because everything that is anything at all must in part determine itself, it to that extent has a power of its own, distinct from every other, even the greatest conceivable. Consequently, all that could be coherently meant by "omnipotence" is all the power that any one thing could be conceived to have, consistently with there being other things having lesser powers over which it alone could be exercised. Supposing, then, that the thing having such omnipotent power were also "omnibeneficent," in the sense of being good for others to an extent than which no greater can be conceived, one would have the essential theistic concept of God as the one thing or individual whose power over others and goodness toward them are not even conceivably surpassable. But even then, one would be forced to conclude that the only possible aim of a God so conceived would not be wholly to determine the decisions of others—since that, not being coherently conceivable, is impossible—but rather, by means of his own free decisions, to optimize the limits of all of theirs. By this I mean that the God whom a process metaphysics allows one to conceive would so act as to set limits to the freedom of others such that, were the limits other than they are, the ratio of opportunity for good to risk of evil would be unfavorable. Thus, if God allowed others either more or less freedom than they actually have, there would be more chances of evil than of good resulting from their decisions, rather than the other way around.

There will be little question in any informed mind that the understanding of God in relation to his creatures that is thus indicated is strikingly different from that of the classical Christian theism which is still widely supposed to be the only metaphysical theism there is. Given the very different metaphysics that such classical theism presupposes, God alone is thought to be self-creative, with everything else being wholly created by him. Thus, according to the classical understanding, God is said to be able to do everything that is not logically self-contradictory, and so his omnipotence is held, in effect, to be all the power there is. Consequently, supposing him also to be omnibeneficent, one has to allow that he can be held accountable for so determining the course of events that there is only good and nothing evil. This explains, of course, why classical Christian theism staggers under the burden of an admittedly insoluable problem of evil. Because its concept of God's omnipotence necessarily implies that God alone is really free and creative, it cannot both admit the reality of evil and still maintain that God is all-good as well as all-powerful, except by the desperate expedient of dignifying what gives every appearance of being a contradiction with the very different connotations of the word "mystery."

To be sure, many classical theologians, past and present, have thought to solve the problem of evil by insisting that man and woman, at least—along, possibly, with such other rational creatures as angels—are genuinely free and self-creative and, therefore, may be charged with responsibility for such evil as undoubtedly exists. Aside from the fact that so-called natural, as distinct from moral, evil is hardly accounted for by such a "free-will defense," there is the serious question of how there can even be such a thing as creaturely freedom, given the insistence of classical theism that God alone is self-creative, and hence possesses all the power there is. In short, even if one grants, as I certainly would, that classical theologians often talk of human freedom, and even of the role of "secondary causes" more generally, there remains ample room to doubt whether they can talk in this way consistently, given what they themselves otherwise assert or imply to be the case.

But, as I have said, there is a second important theological consequence of taking "freedom" to be the key concept of metaphysics. It also follows that *whatever is, even God, is in part determined by the being of other things.* Because anything actual is a creative synthesis of data already given, nothing actual can be the result solely of its own decisions, as distinct from the decisions of others. On the contrary, to be actual at all is to be really, internally related to other things, in the sense that what they are, being synthesized into one's own actuality, thereby partly determines it. But if this is true of all things, just insofar as they are actual, then no actual thing whatever, not even the unsurpassable thing or individual God, can be supposed to fit the classical metaphysical definition of a substance as—in Descartes' formulation—"that which requires nothing but itself in order to exist." As a matter of fact, it is God, least of all, who can be supposed to fit this definition. For if God cannot be conceived as God except he be conceived as the all-perfect or unsurpassable one, the one than whom none greater can be conceived, then the only way to coherently conceive God, assuming that everything actual must be related to other things, is as related to *all* things—as the one individual to whom literally everything makes a difference because it in part determines his own actual being.

That such a universal relativity to all things is indeed a unique property that could not conceivably belong to anyone but God seems clear enough. Just as our own power over others is limited, being power over only *some* others, so it is that only *some* other things have any power over us, in the sense of making any real difference to us by in part determining our actual being. In fact, prior to our birth nothing whatever made any difference to us, and after our death nothing whatever will make any such difference, unless we assume that, in some way or other, we survive our apparent mortality and continue to exist as experiencing subjects. What is more, even of all the things that happen during our lifetime we are effectively touched by hardly any. But it seems just as clear, if you think about it, that a unique individual so radically unlike us as to be effectively touched by literally everything could neither begin nor end (lest he not be touched, after all, by the things occurring either before his beginning or after his end), and, therefore, would be in principle indistinguishable from the unique individual who also effectively touches everything, in that he in part determines the being of all other things by optimizing the limits of their own free decisions. In short, the God whose own actual being literally everything else in part determines is the same God whose existence as such is determined by nothing else, because, as the one unsurpassable individual, his is the one actual being by which literally everything else is also in part determined.

And yet, once again, no one who is well informed would wish to deny that a God so conceived is strikingly different from the God conceived by classical Christian theism. According to the exponents of such theism, present as well as past, God is to be identified metaphysically as the Absolute, which cannot be really or internally related to anything and to which, therefore, literally nothing can make any difference, because it cannot even in part determine the Absolute's actual being. Of course, classical theists, whose metaphysical assumptions require that they conceive God in this way, have nevertheless continued to speak, as religious persons ordinarily do, of God's knowing and loving the world, even as they have continued to say that the whole purpose of man and woman, as well as of the creation generally, is to serve God and live their lives to his glory. But here, too, there is a serious question of consistency—in this case, whether such ordinary religious talk, implying as it all does, that things really do make a difference to God, can even begin to be made consistent with the underlying metaphysical assumptions, which deny that God can be really related to anything whatever and that anything at all can make any difference to him. Moreover, the familiar classical doctrine that such ordinary talk about God has at least a "symbolic" or "analogical" truth is hardly reassuring. For the suspicion remains that the reason God cannot be literally said to know or love the world is that he can be literally said not to do so.

This discussion of the theological consequences of process metaphysics, over against the traditional metaphysics by which so much Christian theology has been shaped, ought to give some idea of why I regard process metaphysics as an indispensable resource for developing an adequate theology of liberation. This discussion should also serve to clarify the essential concepts of the doctrine of God as the ground of freedom, as both the Redeemer and the Emancipator, that I must now try briefly to sketch.

God the Redeemer and the Emancipator

We learned in chapter 2 that the faith which is the existence of freedom is rightly understood as itself the effect of God's grace, in that it is the prevenient action of God's love that is the necessary condition of the possibility of such faith. It should also be clear from what has already been said that the proper theological name for God's love, so far as it is the ground of the possibility of faith, is "redeeming" or "redemptive." God himself, considered in the same respect, is properly said to be "the Redeemer."

The question now is what it is about the very being of God in himself that is properly meant when one speaks in this way. My answer is that theological talk about God as the Redeemer, and hence about his love as redeeming, or the process of redemption, is rightly understood metaphysically when it is taken to refer to the ever-new event of God's own self-creation in response to the free self-creations of all his creatures. In other words, I understand redemption to be the unique process of God's self-actualization, whereby he creatively synthesizes all other things into his own actual being as God.

If one accepts this answer concerning what we mean metaphysically by "redemption," or by "God the Redeemer," there is evidently a sound basis for speaking, at least symbolically or analogically, of the all-embracing love of God. As we ordinarily use the term "love," to love another person is to do something that always has two closely related aspects. First of all, it is to accept the other person, in the sense of taking him or her into account, allowing him or her to make a difference by partly determining one's own actual being. Then, secondly, it is to act toward the other person, in whatever one says or does, on the basis of such acceptance. Accordingly, as different as God's love would certainly have to be from our own, or any other merely creaturely love, it could nevertheless be conceived to be like them in having these same essential aspects: first, the acceptance of others—in God's case, the unlimited acceptance of *all* others—and then, secondly, action directed toward all others on the basis of such unlimited acceptance.

But, clearly, for God thus to accept all of his creatures in the sense of creatively synthesizing all of them into his own everlasting life, is for him to redeem all of his creatures, in that he thereby delivers them from the meaninglessness of not making any difference to anything or anyone more enduring than themselves. This presupposes, naturally, that the defining characteristic of all creaturely existence is its radical contingency—its being such that, although it exists, it need not exist, and might not exist at all. The evidence for this is that there once was when it was not, even as there will be when it will not be anymore. Because it is just such contingency that defines our creaturely existence, the difference that we as creatures can make to one another is always limited by the same radical contingency, which keeps any of us from making more than an extremely limited and short-term difference to those who come after us. If the only contribution our lives could make were the contribution they make to other creaturely lives as limited as our own, they would make no abiding difference and, in that sense, would be meaningless. Death and transience—the perpetual perishing of all things in the ever-rolling stream of time—would be the last word about each of us, and about all of us together.

But if the difference we make is not only such difference as we can make to our fellow creatures but also, and definitively, the difference we each make to God, the one to whom *all* things make a difference and to whose life each thing can contribute *all* that it is, then our lives and all lives are redeemed from meaninglessness by being given an imperishable meaning in the everlasting life of God. In this sense, all things exist, finally, not merely for themselves or for one another, but, as the Christian witness has classically affirmed, for the glory of God, as contributions to his unique and all-encompassing life.

And yet also essential to the historic Christian witness is the promise of redemption from sin, and hence the assertion that God is the Redeemer from sin as well as from death and transience. What does this mean? The essential point is that any talk of sin presupposes the distinctive capacity that makes us human, and that would make any other creature that had it a rational creature like ourselves. I refer to our capacity to be aware in a distinctive way of our own existence and, therewith, of everything else. We not only exist as every other creature does, but we also know that we exist, together with others, in an existing world encompassed by the ultimate mystery whence we all come and whither we all go. This means that to exist in the distinctively human way is always to exist in this knowledge of our own existence, and hence to confront the fundamental option of either accepting ourselves as the creatures we know ourselves to be, or else rejecting ourselves as creatures by trying to deny the fact of our creaturehood. What is properly meant by "sin," in the sense of the word agreeable to the witness of Scripture and the apostles, is not moral transgression, however true it is that such transgression is the inevitable consequence of sin. Rather, sin is just this rejection of ourselves as the creatures we know ourselves to be, the root of which always lies in our having rejected the gift and the demand of the Creator that never cease to encounter us in our awareness of ourselves. In this way, sin at its root is our rejection of God's acceptance of our lives and of all lives, even as faith, as we have seen, is our acceptance of God's acceptance.

Even so, because God's acceptance is boundless, because it is the acceptance of *all* things into his life, it is an acceptance even of sinners, even of those who have rejected his acceptance in rejecting themselves as the creatures they inevitably are. In this sense the love of God, as his ever-renewed act of taking all things into his own everlasting life, is the redemption of his human creatures not only from death and transience, but also from sin.

While *redemption* from sin in one thing, *salvation* from sin is something else. What is properly meant by "salvation" is the process that includes not only the redeeming action of God himself but also the faithful response to this action on the part of the individual sinner. As Augustine put it, "he that made us without ourselves, will not save us without ourselves." We are saved *by* grace—by God's redeeming acceptance of our lives into his, notwithstanding the fact of our sin; but we are saved *through* faith—through our own trusting acceptance of God's acceptance, whereby his redemption of our lives becomes our salvation.

This should suffice to make clear why, in speaking of God as the Redeemer, we are speaking of the ground of our freedom from the bondage of sin, as well as from the bondage of death and transience. But, as we have seen, to exist *in* such freedom is also to exist *for* it, in the case of all the others whose need of redemption is as great as our own. And this means so to exist and act that, in whatever we say or do, we bear witness to them of the redeeming love of God, which is the ground of their freedom from the bondage of sin, as well as from the bondage of transience and death. By thus bearing witness to God as the Redeemer, we ourselves participate in his redeeming work in the only way in which we possibly could participate in it. For redemption as such is God's work alone, our own part therein being but to bear witness to that fact, so that all men and women everywhere may not only be redeemed from death, transience, and sin but also saved from them, in the sense of being freed from the bondage of sin for the freedom of faith.

God's being the ground of freedom, however, is not exhausted by his being the Redeemer, and what we now have to consider is the meaning of the claim that he is also the Emancipator. Here, too, the essential point has already been more or less clearly indicated by my discussion of process metaphysics and, specifically, of its concept of God. It belongs to this concept that God is to be conceived not only as the one to whom all things make a difference—or, in theological terms, as the Redeemer—but also as the one who himself makes a difference to all things, the one whose own self-creation in response to his creatures in part determines all of their self-creations by optimizing the limits of their free decisions. There are the best of reasons for speaking of God as thus partly determining the being of all his creatures simply as the Creator. Given a metaphysics that is at all coherent, the only thing that can be meant, in general, by creating the being of others is so creating oneself as to be part-determinative of the others' own processes of self-creation. Because everything actual is and must be, in part, self-creative, nothing is or can be a creator in the sense of wholly determining what others are to be—even as nothing is or can be a creature in the sense of having its being wholly determined by another. This means, then, that *the* Creator, the one whose creative power over others is such that no greater power can be conceived, can only be the unique individual whose self-creation is part-determinative of the self-creation of *all* others. There is no question, so far as I am concerned, that it is in just this sense that God is, indeed, the Creator and that his creative action in partly determining the being of all other things is simply the other essential aspect of the same all-encompassing love that, in allowing all things to be part-determinative of it, is also uniquely redemptive.

But while I do not have the least hesitation in saying that God is the ground of freedom because he is the Creator as well as the Redeemer, it seems to me illumining to speak of the creative work of God's love as an emancipating, or emancipative, work and of God himself, correspondingly, as the Emancipator. Because the creative work of God is but the other essential aspect of the same unsurpassable love of all others that is also redemptive, his creative power over others is omnibeneficent, or all-good, even as it is omnipotent, or all-powerful. Consequently, God's only aim or intention in exercising his power is the fullest possible self-creation of all his creatures, and so he unfailingly exercises it to optimize the limits of their own free decisions by establishing such fundamental limits of natural order as allow for a greater possibility of good than of evil to be realized through their exercise of freedom. For this reason, God's creative work is, by its very nature, an emancipative work in that it establishes the optimal limits of all his creatures' freedom and thus sets them free to create themselves and one another. This means, among other things, that God's creative or emancipative work is so far from being neutral or indifferent that it "take sides," in the sense that God always acts so as to maximize the opportunities for good, while minimizing the risks of evil. Consequently, even though God's acceptance of others is boundless, his acceptance of everything in no way implies his approval of everything, and his approval of things is, in fact, strictly bounded by the unsurpassable goodness of his aim.

Thus to say that God is the ground of freedom because he is the Emancipator as well as the Redeemer is to speak of the creative, and hence the emancipative aspect of his love, whereby he intends the fullest possible self-realization of each of his creatures and infallibly acts to do all that can be done to that end—save only what his creatures themselves have to do, both for themselves and for one another. And this, of course, is why there is a very important difference between the way in which we can participate in God's redemptive work and the way in which we can participate in his emancipative work. Whereas redemption as such, as distinct from salvation, is God's work alone, in which we are able to participate only by bearing witness to it, emancipation is the work of God in which he is dependent on the co-operation of his creatures if the intention lying behind it is to be fully realized.

Needless to say, God has his own unsurpassable part to play in this emancipative work, in playing which he is not in the least dependent upon anyone. To this extent the other half of Augustine's statement is also true, that the God who will not save us without ourselves nevertheless makes us without ourselves. God makes us without ourselves, namely, because the fact that there is some world for us and our fellow creatures to exist and to act in is no more our own doing than is the fact that there is always a certain relatively fixed and stable order to the world which allows for the possibility of more good than evil being realized through exercising our creaturely freedom. All this is solely God's work, in no way anything that either we or any other creature could even possibly do. But since not even God can wholly determine the being of others, each of them being, if actual at all, in part self-determined, the details of the world that exists and the local orders that come to prevail within the larger, cosmic order that God alone establishes are all co-determined by the creatures themselves, by their own processes of self-creation and, thereby, creation of one another. To this not inconsiderable extent, we participate in

God's emancipating work of optimizing the limits of creaturely freedom only insofar as we do our own irreplaceable part in realizing the aim by which God's unique part in this work is guided. Accordingly, we may say that, even as God will not save us without ourselves, so he will not emancipate us without ourselves—nor will he emancipate others without our participation in his emancipating work of establishing the optimal conditions of their freedom.

This leads to the important question of just how we go about participating in God's emancipating work. If we recall what was said in the preceding chapter, the first thing to say, obviously, is that optimizing the limits of freedom, which is one and the same with bearing witness to God's love, consists in so speaking and acting in relation to others as to respond to all their creaturely needs. But as helpful as this no doubt is as a general answer to the question, it fails to take account of the important fact that creaturely needs are by no means all on the same level. The deeper need of any creature, apart from such need as it may feel for redemption from death and transience and salvation from sin, is the need to exist in a world sufficiently ordered to permit it to realize its own fullest potentialities. Just because this is so, however, it would seem that we participate in God's emancipative work not only, or primarily, by responding to particular creaturely needs arising within the existing world but also, and crucially, by responding to the need of each creature that the existing world itself permit the optimal exercise of its own freedom of self-creation. I take it that this is the point Gustavo Gutierrez wants to make when he says that "the poor person is the by-product of the system in which we live and for which we are responsible. He is the oppressed, the exploited, the proletarian, the one deprived of the fruit of his labor and despoiled of being a person. For that reason, the poverty of the poor person is not a call for a generous act which will alleviate his misery, but rather a demand for building a different social order."[7]

At any rate, I maintain that, even as God's own emancipating work consists in meeting this deeper creaturely need for a world in which one can freely determine one's own destiny in solidarity with one's fellow creatures, so, too, must the crucial part of our participation in God's emancipating work consist in efforts to respond to this same deeper need—the essential difference between God's part in such work and our own being that he establishes the larger, *cosmic* order of nature, while we are responsible for establishing the smaller, *local* orders that we properly speak of as "societies" and "cultures." This is my way of formulating the essential insight both of the earlier social gospel and of the liberation theologies of our own day. For I, too, wish to claim that by far the most important way in which we participate in God's work of emancipation is to labor for fundamental social and cultural change—the kind of structural or systemic change in the very order of our society and culture that is clearly necessary if each and every person is to be the active subject of his or her history instead of merely its passive object.

Of course, to speak of the necessity of fundamental change is to acknowledge the inequality and injustice of the existing social and cultural order and, therewith, the necessarily conflictive character of our existence in it. But even as God is not neutral or indifferent to creaturely conflict but always sides with what makes for the good of his creatures as against all that makes for evil, so we, too, cannot avoid the conflict of human interests or evade the demand always to take sides with the oppressed against all who oppress them. Nor can we ever rule out the eventuality that we can be obedient to this demand only by using force to oppose those who forcibly destroy the conditions of others' freedom—although we will more likely judge rightly in the whole matter of using force if we recall that, for God and, in a radically more limited way, for anyone else who loves, all opposition to others' interests is an opposition to one's own. Just to the extent of one's love for others, one can oppose them only by opposing something in oneself. The essential point, in any case, is that we can participate in the emancipative work of God only by sharing fully in the conflict of human interests and in the struggle to build a more just and equitable social and cultural order.

In conclusion, I would make two related comments. If one approaches the task of a theology of liberation as I have tried to do in these last two chapters, it is essential to recognize the systematic ambiguity of the term "liberation." By this I mean that this term may be quite properly used in different contexts of meaning to refer to two distinct and, in fact, very different things—namely, redemption and emancipation. To identify these in any way, or to fail consistently to distinguish between them, is to confuse the emancipative work of God with his redemptive work, the Emancipator with the Redeemer. But just as essential is to recognize that it is *one* God who alone is both Redeemer *and* Emancipator and who, therefore, is the one ultimate ground of our freedom and of the freedom of everyone else. Consequently, to separate emancipation and redemption in any way, or to play them off against one another, is to deny that both are the work of one and the same divine love, and that it is always in both, in their distinct but always integrally related ways, that each of us is given and called to share.

CHAPTER 4

SUBTLER FORMS OF BONDAGE & LIBERATION

If the preceding chapters have succeeded in their purpose, we have now taken two important steps toward a theology of liberation. One such step is to have understood the systematic ambiguity of the concept "liberation," which requires that we distinguish without separating, or that we relate without identifying, the two processes that I have called redemption and emancipation. Both of these processes are quite properly included under the one concept "liberation," because the one as well as the other involves a process of being liberated from bondage. In the case of redemption, it is liberation from the bondage of death, transience, and sin; in the case of emancipation, it is liberation from all the other forms of bondage, particularly the structural or systemic bondage, that keep us and our fellow creatures from realizing our fullest potentialities. But while there is thus a single process of liberation embracing both redemption and emancipation, these two processes are sufficiently distinct from one another that only serious confusion can result from simply identifying them.

This became all the clearer as we took the other important step of explicating the ultimate ground of freedom in the being of God in himself. Although there is indeed one God who is the sole ultimate ground of all freedom, and hence of both processes of liberation, that one God is properly distinguished as both the Emancipator and the Redeemer—his emancipative and redemptive work being two quite different, even if integrally related, aspects of the one divine reality of all-embracing love. Thus if God as the Redeemer so acts as to accept all things into his own life, where they alone have an abiding meaning, God as the Emancipator so acts as to optimize the limits of freedom for the self-creations of all his creatures.

Grounded as it is, then, in the dipolar nature of God's own being, the distinction between redemption and emancipation is absolutely fundamental to any adequate theology of liberation. Just as fundamental, however, is that both processes are so grounded in the one being of God that neither they nor our own participation in them can ever be separated or played off against one another. The one liberating work of God, in which each of us is given and called to play our part, is a redeeming *and* an emancipating work.

Beyond this fundamental understanding of faith and freedom and of their ultimate ground in the liberating love of God, there is yet a further step I should like to take toward a theology of liberation. I made the statement earlier that the forms of human bondage are necessarily multiple and that there are yet subtler forms than those that ordinarily claim our attention. Among the other things I had in mind in saying this are certain constraints that, as it seems to me, usually keep the whole project of a theology of liberation itself from ever being adequately realized.

One such constraint I drew attention to in the preceding chapter, when I alluded to the widely held assumption that the only terms in which the being of God in himself can be explicated meta-physically are the terms provided by classical Christian theism. Whether this assumption is made explicitly or only tacitly, making it delimits one's choices either to a metaphysical understanding of God that is profoundly alien to the whole idea of human liberation or else to a theology that settles for thinking and speaking simply of the meaning of God for us, as distinct from the being of God in himself. Consequently, to point to an alternative metaphysi-cal theism, as I sought to do in that same chapter, is, in effect, to emancipate theological reflection from the narrow range of alternatives between which it is supposedly constrained to choose.

But if I am right, there are certain other, subtler forms of bondage from which theology must also be emancipated if anything like an adequate theology of liberation is to be achieved. Therefore, it is some of these subtler forms of bondage and emancipation that I wish to consider in this concluding chap-ter—keeping firmly in mind in doing so that here, too, our task is not to develop one theology of liberation among others but rather to move toward such a theology by clarifying what it would necessarily have to share in common with any other that was at all adequate.

Beyond Homocentrism

One of the characteristics of situations of inequality is that it is solely by the standards of the haves that the have-nots tend to measure their disadvantage. Thus, for example, students of American history have pointed out that the political achievement of Andrew Jackson was to bring a class to power that, while poorer than the Whig aristocrats of the time, was just as eager to get rich quickly, and every bit as committed to economic expansion as the way to do so. Accordingly, in the battle Jackson waged with the Bank of the United States for cheap credit as a means to such expansion, what was resented by those whose cause he represented was not at all the wealth of the rich but only their exclusiveness. The common enemy of Whig and Democrat alike was whoever stood in the way of economic growth. As it turned out, that common enemy was the native American. And so the other side of the much-vaunted triumph of the common man through Jacksonian democracy was "the trail of tears" of the Cherokee nation.

Victor C. Ferkiss, to whom I owe this first example, gives yet another from American history when he speaks of the failure at the end of the nineteenth century of such movements as Henry George's Single Tax movement and Edward Bellamy's Nationalism. Their failure, he argues, was largely due to the fact that they, and even the once-promising American Socialist party, were not protests against liberal society as such, insofar as their supporters were concerned, but rather the complaint of those excluded from the division of the booty—Jacksonianism in a new guise. As soon as new ships to loot hove into view and new towns were found to sack these movements faded away, though it took the repression of the Wilson Administration during World War I to finally destroy the Socialists as a significant political force. Everyone save a few isolated intellectuals—men like pioneer ecologist George Perkins Marsh, naturalist John Muir, or government scientist and explorer John Wesley Powell—unreservedly embraced liberalism and its doctrine of the acquisition of wealth through the ruthless exploitation of nature.[8]

This second example, especially, illumines one of the subtler forms of bondage from which, as I see it, theology today needs to be emancipated if there is ever to be anything like an adequate theology of liberation. I refer to the exaggerated humanism, or homocentrism, for which the larger world of nature is, in effect, the common enemy of the most varied human groups, advantaged and disadvantaged alike. If such homocentrism, with its presupposed dualism of history and nature, has been a defining characteristic of modern Western culture generally, it has also been typical of the whole movement of liberal theology that has sought to come to terms with modern culture in reflecting critically on the traditional forms of the Christian witness. It is not surprising, then, if we recall that it is to just this larger liberal theological movement that the various theologies of liberation also belong, that they, too, should be marked by the same homocentrism. Whatever the form of bondage to which they may be oriented—political, economic, cultural, racial, or sexual—it is solely with *human* liberation that they are typically concerned, and if they regard non-human nature as having any value at all, it is the strictly instrumental value it has for realizing *human* potentialities.

That this is so will seem all the more understandable if we remind ourselves that homocentrism in this sense cuts across even extreme differences between alternative understandings of human existence in the contemporary world. Broadly speaking, one may say that, aside from the older understandings mediated by the Christian and other religious traditions, these alternatives include two main types of post-Christian humanism: an older, more evolutionary type, with its ideology of economic growth through science and technology, typical of the highly industrialized societies of the West; and a newer, more revolutionary type, with its ideology of overcoming oppression through the overthrow of the existing order, typical of the other highly developed societies of the East. And yet, as different as these two types of contemporary humanism certainly are, there are many respects in which they are similar, and none is more striking than their respective understandings of the place and value of nonhuman nature.

For the older, more evolutionary type of humanism, from Bacon and Locke all the way down to the theorists and policymakers of capitalist societies today, nature is understood as having, or, rather, acquiring, value solely through human beings. Lacking in any intrinsic worth of its own, it exists entirely in order to be exploited by human ingenuity and industry in that acquisition of wealth which is the necessary condition of economic growth, and hence of human fulfillment. Nuances aside, however, nature is hardly understood any differently by the other more revolutionary type of humanism, whether by such classical spokesmen as Marx or by the theorists and politicians of contemporary socialism. Despite Marx's occasional charge that capitalism alienates human beings not only from themselves and one another but also from the nature around them, even he typically assumes that man is the measure of all things and nature an enemy to be conquered. Indeed, Marx understands the conquest of nature through science and technology to be a precondition for realizing the kingdom of freedom. And so socialists today, true to their Marxist heritage, typically share the older liberal goal of unlimited economic growth through science and technology. The gravamen of their complaint against capitalism is simply that its pursuit of private profit now tends rather to inhibit than to promote the technological triumph of man over nature to which socialism itself is wholeheartedly committed.

There is nothing in the least strange, then, about the homocentrism that is so prominent a feature of the theologies of liberation. For from one extreme to the other, this same homocentrism characterizes the whole spectrum of the contemporary humanisms with which, in one way or another, each of these theologies is a piece.

Nor is this all that can be said by way of explaining the typical homocentrism of theologies of liberation, as well as of modern Christian theology generally. It is widely agreed that both of the main types of contemporary humanism are properly said to be "post-Christian" in that they both represent a secularization of the understanding of human existence characteristic of Christianity. Consequently, there are those who have argued that it is Christianity itself, or the Judaeo-Christian tradition more generally, that is the original source of the homocentrism of modern Western culture. In the form in which this argument has sometimes been stated, it may be easily criticized as simplistic by pointing to a good deal of evidence that tells against it. Since it is precisely the more modern expressions of Christianity that are notably homocentric, it is a fair question whether the homocentrism of modernity is the effect of Christian homocentrism or, rather, its cause.

And yet it would be mistaken, in my judgment, simply to dismiss the argument that traditional Christianity has been important in developing the modern dualism of history and nature and its homocentric understanding of human liberation. Not the least reason for saying this is the position taken by certain Christian apologists in the face of criticisms of Christianity that have been made in recent years by a number of persons concerned with our growing ecological crisis. According to these apologists, it is not possible to avoid such criticisms by denying the difference in principle between nature in general and human existence in particular, or by so expanding the concepts of ethics as to allow rights to nature that human beings have the responsibility to respect. On the contrary, by these apologists' own account, biblical religion and theology are sufficiently homocentric to require the differentiation of man as in an important respect "a non-natural creature" and to preclude assigning enough intrinsic value to anything else in nature to entitle it to be the bearer of even the least right of its own.[9] That at least some Christian theologians should find it possible as well as necessary thus to defend an "open, unabashed anthropocentrism" is surely some reason for thinking that theology's bondage to such an anthropocentrism is not merely a function of its alliance with one form or another of modern humanism.

Nevertheless, I am convinced that bondage is

exactly what it is and that theology today both must and can be freed of it.

Theology *must* be freed from such homocentrism because, unless and until it is, it cannot possibly be an adequate theology in either of the respects in which it is called to be so. It cannot be adequate in respect of being understandable to human beings today, because, if anything is now understood, it is that the dualism of history and nature presupposed by such homocentrism is both theoretically false and practically vicious. There is every reason to believe that human existence has emerged from nature and is itself entirely natural. Its most distinctive characteristics, such as the capacity for true speech and self-consciousness, realize some of nature's own potentialities, instead of in any way distinguishing it as "non-natural." In fact, so far from indicating that man and woman in any way stand apart from nature and above it, human culture and history are one way—the distinctively human way—of being natural. This means, among other things, that they are subject to the same laws of ecology as apply throughout the ecosphere of nature generally—such laws as that everything is connected with everything else, everything must go somewhere, everything is gained at some cost, and so on. To continue to speak, therefore, as some theologians do, of "nature's hostile territory," and thus to claim that "man is emancipated *from* nature *for* history," is to foster the very attitudes toward our natural environment that have already driven us to the brink of historical catastrophe, whether through the exhaustion of nonrenewable resources upon which any progress in history is dependent or through so polluting our natural home that it is no longer humanly habitable.

A theology bound to such homocentrism can just as little be adequate in respect of being appropriate to the Christian witness of faith itself. Whatever some theologians may say, and however much in the Christian tradition may appear to bear them out, I am persuaded that the most fundamental axioms of biblical faith preclude any such dualism between nature and history. One reason for this is that careful scholars of the creation narratives in Genesis persuasively argue that these narratives are witnesses as much to the essential unity of man and woman with all their fellow creatures as to their unique difference over against them. Thus Claus Westermann points out that "the animals receive the first blessing mentioned in the Bible," and "the same words spoken to the animals, 'be fruitful and multiply' are used . . . to convey God's blessing to man. . . . This connection between the animals and man . . . is a stronger statement concerning the common relationship between man and the animals than is the assumption of genealogical connections in a theory of evolution."[10]

The crucial reasons for my persuasion, however, in no way depend on the exegesis of particular

passages of Scripture, but have to do with the
necessary conditions of the possibility of the entire
scriptural witness and, in that sense, with what I
have referred to as the axioms of biblical faith.
Among such axioms, as classical Christian theology
rightly recognized, is that not only man and woman
but anything whatever is created out of nothing by
God, and hence to some degree or other displays the
being of its Creator, who is immanent in it as well as
transcendent of it. This implies that, while there is
an *infinite* difference between God and every
creature, there neither is nor could be an *absolute*
difference between God and any creature, from
which it follows that any difference between
creatures themselves, even the unique difference
between human creatures and all the others, is and
must be a merely *finite* difference. Hence if,
according to Scripture, all other creatures are to be
loved, finally, solely for the sake of God, then the
same is true of human creatures, who are likewise to
be loved, finally, solely to God's glory. On the other
hand, if God is immanent in human creatures so
that, displaying the being of their Creator, they are
the bearers of rights that should be respected, then
the same is true of all other creatures, each of whom
in its own way and to its own degree also displays
the being of the Creator, thereby acquiring the
intrinsic worth that is the basis of all rights.

Given the scriptural axiom of creation, then, the
dominion over the other creatures to which man and

woman are uniquely appointed is by no means a matter simply of their stewardship over a nature having merely instrumental value for human history. On the contrary, they are most like the God in whose image they are uniquely created when they so rule over creation as to recognize not only the *difference* in intrinsic value between one kind of creature and another, but also the *unity* in intrinsic value by which all creatures are bound together as the good creation of God.

But if theology must be freed from homocentrism to be either appropriate or understandable, it also *can* be freed from homocentrism because there are conceptual resources available for overcoming all dualism by expressing just this combination of unity and difference between nature and history. That this is so should be evident from my argument in the last chapter that process metaphysics is the consistent and thoroughgoing generalization of the key concept of "freedom." If, as such metaphysics maintains, to be anything actual at all is to be in part self-creative, and hence an instance of freedom, then even the least actual thing must bear at least some likeness to the eminent freedom of God, who, as the greatest conceivable instance of self-creation, is immanent in all other instances as well as transcendent of them. But this evidently implies, in turn, that anything actual has at least some intrinsic value and that any difference between one kind of actuality and another is at most a finite difference between emergent levels of value corresponding to different emergent levels of freedom. At the same time, a process metaphysics such as this has all the resources necessary for conceptualizing the real uniqueness of human existence. For although there is only a finite difference between human existence and all the other kinds of actual things, human freedom and value are nevertheless emergent properties of a distinctive level of natural existence and as such are irreducible to those of any lower level. In short, just as process metaphysics frees us to talk about the being of God in himself as the ground of freedom, so it also provides the concepts by which we can at last go beyond homocentrism in our understanding of human liberation.

The objection that is certain to be made to this argument is that such a nonhomocentric understanding of liberation is self-defeating. By insisting on the unity of history and nature and the intrinsic value of every creature, it relativizes our proper concern with the liberation of men and women, especially their emancipation from the forms of structural or systemic bondage from which so many of them unjustly suffer. That this, at any rate, is the inherent danger of such an understanding is clear from the fact that much of the recent environmental movement has displayed such an indifference to the demands of social justice that there are grounds for suspecting that it functions as an ideology, as a means employed by the more highly developed societies to discourage the growth of those that are far less so.

My response to this objection is to say, first of all, that I have no intention whatever of playing off a concern for the fulfillment of nature generally against a concern for social justice. To argue, as I have, that every creature on earth has some intrinsic value and, to that extent, deserves to be respected is in no way to imply that all creatures have an equal value or that there are not important differences between the rights of one creature and another. But I find not the least reason to believe, as so many seem to do, that human creatures can be treated as ends in themselves, and hence as more than mere means, only if the rest of earth's creatures cannot. On the contrary, I entirely share the judgment of those who see the closest connections between our treatment of nature generally as mere means and our treatment of our fellow human beings in exactly the same way. From all the evidence known to me, the history of our species' ruthless exploitation of other species is entirely of a piece with the history of our ruthless exploitation of one another. Therefore, I can only agree with Charles Birch when, in replying to much the same kind of objection, he insists that the increasingly negative impact of human beings on the natural environment through ever-expanding growth of population, consumption of resources, and environmental deterioration is directly con- nected with the persistence of radical inequality between the rich nations and the poor. As he puts it: "There is no chance of the poor countries developing adequately unless the rich countries reduce the huge proportion they contribute to the total impact. This involves a programme of de-development of the rich world. The rich must live more simply that the poor may simply live."[11]

Beyond this, my response to the objection is to say that any theology worthy of the name must be just as concerned with questions of truth as with issues of justice, if only because the only way in which justice in the long run can be achieved is on the basis of truth. If it is correct to argue, as I have, that modern homocentrism is true neither to the scriptural axiom of the creation of all things by God nor to the best insights of contemporary science and philosophy, then theology has every reason to go beyond such homocentrism even if it also has reason to see that the truth of human solidarity with nature is kept free from ideological misuse. Indeed, any other course would be profoundly unjust to human beings, who have everything to gain from being emancipated from supportive illusions about their own specialness. For it is only so that they may fully assume that dominion over the creation to which they are appointed in being called to rule over their fellow creatures after the image of God's own loving rule—so as not merely to use and to exploit them but also to enjoy and to further them as co-participants in the all-inclusive end of God's reign.

The Emancipation of Theology

These last comments lead naturally to the other point I wish to make in this concluding chapter. Although I have already been speaking about the emancipation of theology from its bondage to homocentrism, it will have become clear that, as subtle as this form of bondage may be, it is by no means peculiar to theology, much less to the already existing theologies of liberation. So far as modern Western culture is concerned, at any rate, such homocentrism is so pervasive that it has not been until relatively recently, in the face of the mounting ecological crisis, that most of us have even become aware of the extent of our bondage to it. Because this is so, all that I have said about going beyond homocentrism, although applied to theology, admits of a much wider application. Indeed, it applies wherever the truth of our human solidarity with other creatures and our responsibility for them is ignored or denied, whether expressly or by implication. But it is quite otherwise with what I take to be an even subtler form of bondage from which theology both must and can be freed if there is ever to be an adequate theology of liberation. In this case, the bondage in question is peculiar to theology, and to speak of emancipation from it, as I now propose to do, is to speak precisely and only of the emancipation of theology.

The form of bondage of which I speak may be

indicated by saying that, throughout its history right up to the present time, theology has been understood and done rather as a form of rationalization than as a form of critical reflection. This is to assume, of course, the usual, pejorative sense of the term "rationalization," according to which it designates the process of giving reasons for positions already taken as distinct from the process of determining in a reasoned way whether the positions already taken are, in fact, worth taking. It will be recalled that, in discussing earlier what is properly meant by "critical reflection," I defined it as the process of determining in a deliberate, methodical, and reasoned way whether something that appears to be the case, or, alternatively, is said to be the case, really is so. But it is precisely not critical reflection in this sense, but, rather, what I have distinguished as rationalization that has almost always been taken to be the proper business of Christian theology. If theology has been conceived to have any properly critical function at all, it has been restricted to criticizing particular witnesses of faith by reference to whatever has been understood to constitute normative Christian witness, whether Scripture and tradition, or, rather, Scripture alone.

To be sure, there has been the important difference between classical Roman Catholic and classical Protestant theology that, whereas the former has been understood to have the task of rationalizing the positions taken by a particular institutional church (namely, the Roman Catholic Church), the latter has been expected to rationalize the positions of that visible church which, being always only more or less visible in the various institutional churches, can never be simply identified with any of them. Notwithstanding this difference, however, in neither case has theology been allowed, much less assigned, the task of critically reflecting on the positions taken by the church in such a way as to ask and answer the radical question as to their truth. On the contrary, theology has been, and, for the most part, still is expected simply to assume the truth of the church's positions and then to occupy itself with giving reasons for them—just this being the sense almost always given to Anselm's famous phrase, taken as describing theology's task: "faith seeking understanding" *(fides quaerens intellectum).*

Of course, this classical understanding of theology has long since been revised by what I have spoken of as liberal theology. Insisting that human experience and reason are also criteria of religious and theological truth, liberal theologians have never been content simply to rationalize positions already taken in the historic Christian witness, but have criticized those positions on the basis of others typically taken by persons sharing in the experience and reflection distinctive of modern Western culture. But even with this liberal revision, the task of theology, significantly, has still been understood less as critical reflection than as rationalization—with the single, if important, difference that the positions to be rationalized by theology have been those of modern secularity as well as those of historic Christianity. Indeed, liberal theologians have typically understood theology as a rationalization of the Christian witness in terms of secular concerns and questions. If they have also sought to deepen secularity by interpreting it, in turn, in terms of the Christian witness, they have nevertheless conceived of their efforts as originating in a prior option and commitment to secular self-understanding.

There is no need to repeat here what I said in chapter 1 about the self-criticism of liberal theology effected subsequently by so-called neo-orthodoxy, or about theology's having more recently passed into a genuinely postliberal phase. The pertinent point is simply that, even in these later developments, theology has continued to be understood and done for the most part as the rationalization of positions already taken, rather than as critical reflection on the worth of such positions. Thus whether the positions in question have been solely those of "the biblical message," as in neo-orthodoxy, or, rather, also those of contemporary secularity, as in much of the postliberal theology of the present time, in either case theology has been conceived as reflection on the basis of such positions instead of reflection directed toward critically establishing their truth.

The even more pertinent point is that the same is true of the concept of theology's task typically expressed or implied by the theologies of liberation. From their standpoint, naturally, all the other ways of understanding and doing theology are more or less seriously inadequate. In fact, they commonly charge that not only classical theology and its liberal revision, but also neo-orthodoxy and the postliberal theology of the present all either are or are in danger of becoming "ideological" in the Marxist sense of the word. The grounds for this charge are that these theologies are all rationalizations of positions already taken either in the historic Christian witness or in modern secularity. As such, they either set forth an abstract understanding of redemption having no positive relation to the concrete tasks of emancipation (as tends to be true of classical and neo-orthodox theologies) or else (as in the more liberal and postliberal theologies) they speak of emancipation itself in purely abstract terms, ignoring the basic inequalities between different classes and societies and the radically conflictive character of our actual, concrete history. Thus a constant theme in all the theologies of liberation that are at all methodologically self-conscious is the need for "the liberation of theology," by which they mean the emancipation of theology itself from any such ideological function or misuse. This emancipation can be effected, they urge, only insofar as the prior option and commitment from which theology is done are not simply a believing acceptance of the Christian witness, or even that together with a commitment to secularity, but also a real and effective solidarity with the oppressed, whether they be exploited nations and classes, despised cultures, or discriminated races and sexes. Only when theology is a reflection in and on the actual praxis of emancipation from these kinds of structural bondage—or, in other words, only when theology is a rationalization of just such praxis—can it itself be freed from either being a mere ideology or being misused as one.

But now, from my standpoint, this proposal for the liberation of theology is not really anything of the kind. It is simply one more proposal for the bondage of theology, because on it, no less than on all the earlier understandings, theology remains the rationalization of certain positions instead of being critical reflection on their meaning and truth. It is true that the terms of the bondage are different; and, assuming, as I have argued, that existence in faith is existence for the freedom of others, and so participation in God's emancipating as well as in his redeeming work, one might well prefer bondage on these terms to any others. But bondage it nonetheless is, and if theology otherwise is open to the charge of ideology, this charge is hardly rendered groundless simply because the positions theology rationalizes are those of the oppressed instead of the oppressors. Indeed, the endemic danger of any such theology is that it will finally be little more than the rationalization of these positions, since it is solely in terms of them that it rationalizes the positions of the Christian witness of faith. Thus, according to one liberation theologian, "Christians should not redefine social praxis by starting with the gospel message. They should do just the opposite. They should seek out the historical import of the gospel by starting with social praxis."[12] That the motives behind such a statement may be of the best, or that one may share the same social and political sympathies as the person making it, ought not to obscure the fact that the one-sided method it recommends could no more be accepted by an adequate Christian theology than the one-sided method it opposes.

Consequently, my own proposal for the emancipation of theology is quite different. Because the real root of theology's historic bondage is the underlying conception of its task as the rationalization of positions already taken, the only way in which it can be emancipated is by reconceiving its task, instead, as the critical reflection on such positions. Only insofar as theology is consistently conceived as such reflection—on the positions taken in the normative Christian witness as well as on those taken by men and women today in their actual conflictive history—can it be said that theology really is free.

Of course, in order to be such critical reflection, theology has to be governed by certain criteria. But as difficult as it may be to specify just what theology's criteria require in a given situation, there surely can be little question about the criteria themselves. They are the very same criteria of appropriateness and understandability that I have spoken of all along. Theology can judge no position to be adequate that is not at once appropriate to the Christian witness as judged by its apostolic norm, and understandable to human existence as judged in terms of common experience and reason. Because these criteria are not in serious question, there is no reason to doubt that theology not only must but also can be freed from its historic bondage. For if these criteria are a *necessary* condition of theology's being critical reflection instead of mere rationalization, they are also a *sufficient* condition, in that the emancipation of theology can always be effected, provided only that it reflect on all positions in terms of these criteria, and judge no position to be adequate unless it satisfies the requirements of both of them.

The point in urging this proposal, naturally, is in no way to suggest that theology itself ought not to take any positions. The idea of a theology that would be neutral in that sense is absurd. But far from absurd is the idea of a theology that would take the positions it takes only on the basis of a critical reflection governed by the two criteria of appropriateness and understandability. In fact, I am quite convinced that this is the only idea of theology as itself radically free, in the twofold sense of being free *for* all positions precisely because it is also free *from* all positions.

The clear implication of this idea, however, is that the only way in which theology as such can be of service to any emancipating praxis is by critically reflecting on its positions in terms of these same criteria. While theological reflection is always free to *result* in positions reflecting the closest solidarity with the oppressed over against their oppressors, it is not in this solidarity, or in the praxis expressive of it, that theology *originates.* On the contrary, the prior option and commitment from which theology springs are simply the prior option and commitment of any and all critical reflection—namely, human existence as such in its profound exigency for the truth that alone can make us free. It is because theology as such exists, above all, to respond to this deep human need for truth that its service to the praxis of emancipation can be only the *indirect* service of critically reflecting on the positions that such praxis implies. The whole point on which I have been insisting, however, is that this is the only service that a truly free theology is in a position to perform.

There will be some, I am sure, for whom this conclusion provokes the question whether the emancipation of theology for which I am calling is, after all, a good thing. But once this question is clearly raised, there can be little doubt about the answer. Whatever else theology may be said to be from the standpoint of Christian faith and witness, it is itself one of the ways in which we as Christians are called to bear witness to our faith—not only by *what* we think and say theologically but also, and no less importantly, by *how* we think and say it. Thus not the least way of attesting one's belief that we are saved, not by our own good works, but solely by the grace of God accepted in faith is to be willing to subject all of one's positions, *including this very belief,* to critical reflection, thereby acknowledging that they are, at best, but our own intellectual good works. To become clear about this, however, is to realize that any theology other than one that is itself genuinely free can hardly bear witness to a God whose gift and demand are radical freedom. Indeed, there must be something strangely contradictory about a theology that explicitly talks about liberation only in such a way as to implicitly attest to its own bondage.

Accordingly, not the least important step we have to take if we would really move toward a theology of liberation is to emancipate theology from its historic bondage as mere rationalization to its proper freedom as critical reflection. To stop short of such emancipation would be to settle for a theology that could not possibly be an adequate theology of liberation, for it could do justice neither to the deep human aspiration to be free nor to the witness of faith that promises to satisfy that aspiration.

NOTES

1. James H. Cone, "Black Power, Black Theology, and the Study of Theology and Ethics," *Theological Education, 6 (1970) 209.*

2. Vivian Gornick, *The Romance of American Communism* (New York: Basic Books, 1978); quoted in *Time,* February 6 (1978) 90.

3. See Willi Marxsen, *The New Testament as the Church's Book,* trans. James E. Mignard (Philadelphia: Fortress Press, 1972), pp. 64-128.

4. *Luther's Works,* 31, ed. Harold J. Grimm (Philadelphia: Muhlenberg Press, 1957), p. 344.

5. Alexander Miller, *The Renewal of Man: A Twentieth Century Essay on Justification by Faith* (Garden City, N.Y.: Doubleday & Co., 1955), p. 126.

6. Juan Luis Segundo, *Our Idea of God,* trans. John Drury (Maryknoll, N. Y.: Orbis Books, 1974).

7. Gustavo Gutierrez, "Faith as Freedom: Solidarity with the Alienated and Confidence in the Future," in *Living with Change, Experience, Faith,* ed. Francis A. Eigo (Villanova, Pa.: Villanova University Press, 1976), p. 25.

8. Victor C. Ferkiss, *The Future of Technological Civilization* (New York: George Braziller, 1974), p. 42; cf. also pp. 36-37.

9. Thomas Siger Derr, *Ecology and Human Liberation: A Theological Critique of the Use and Abuse of Our Birthright* (Geneva: WSCF Books, 1973), p. 40. Quotations in subsequent paragraphs expressing the same point of view are all also from this book (pp. 46, 53), which has been published in another edition as *Ecology and Human Need* (Philadelphia: The Westminster Press, 1975).

10. Claus Westermann, *The Genesis Accounts of Creation,* trans. Norman E. Wagner (Philadelphia: Fortress Press, 1964), pp. 19-20.

11. Charles Birch, "Creation, Technology and Human

Survival: Called to Replenish the Earth," *The Ecumenical Review,* 28 (1976) 70.
12. J. P. Richard; quoted in Juan Luis Segundo, *The Liberation of Theology,* trans. John Drury (Maryknoll, N.Y.: Orbis Books, 1976), p. 85.